1- 16-75

How To Fix It

**An Illustrated Step-by-Step Guide to Home Repairs
For the Woman who Wants to Fix It Now**

How
To Fix It

by Ann Singerie

Doubleday and Company Inc.,
Garden City, New York 1974

Series Coordinator: John Mason
Design Director: Guenther Radtke
Picture Editor: Peter Cook
Copy Editor: Mitzi Bales
Research: Nina Sklansky
        Elizabeth Lake
Consultants: Beppie Harrison
           Jo Sandilands

This edition published in the
United States of America in 1974 by
Doubleday & Company Inc., New York
in association with Aldus Books Limited

Library of Congress Catalog
No. 74 4165

ISBN 0 385 09756 5

Printed and bound in Yugoslavia by
Mladinska Knjiga, Ljubljana

Contents

Have you ever been faced with a washer that won't wash, or a drain that won't drain? What do you do when your door-bell won't ring, your toilet won't stop running, or your car won't start. If, like so many women, you're stumped by fixit problems, this is the book for you. Starting with descriptions of basic tools and how to use them, it provides guidance on a wide range of home repairs—from putting up bookshelves for convenience and ap-pearance, to saving your favorite lamp by replacing its socket. A final section deals thoroughly with routine maintenance around the home, telling you both when you have to give up and call repairmen, and what to do in an emergency. This is a book, then, that will not only save your temper, but also your budget.

Who Runs This Place?

For many long centuries, it has been up to the woman to see that the entire household—small, medium, or large—runs smoothly.

Below: the medieval lady of the manor had heavy responsibilities of money and personnel management, and it left her little leisure.

Right: in 17th-century Spain—as elsewhere and later—the old cook served faithfully.

Right: even after slavery had ended, the black woman of the South was bound to domestic service. Her skill as a cook, and her role as Mammy, were almost legendary.

Below: it took a huge staff of servants, who worked hard and long, to keep the large homes of well-to-do Victorians going well.

Above and below: today's housewife usually has labor-saving aids instead of servants. When one of these complicated machines go wrong, as they often can do, she is in trouble.

How Did We Do Without Them?

We so take modern plumbing and lighting for granted that it's hard to believe they are something less than a hundred years old.

Below: the unsanitary, unsafe London of the 1700's—a chamber pot emptied on someone's head, a hazardous shave by candlelight, and only a hand-held lantern for street lights.

Right: the floating wick in oil, an early form of lamp, didn't cast very much light.

Above: though this lamp of 1793 gave better light, it was still little enough for close work.

Right: in a publicity stunt in the later 1800's, Thomas Edison used electricity to light up the hat of a man passing out ads.

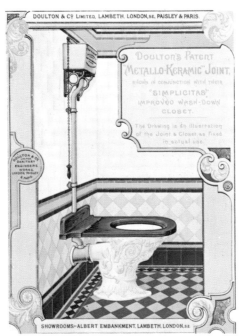

Above: Victorian advances in sanitation brought us a bathtub and toilet very like those of today, but the shower-bath operated by foot (top right) was more a gimmick.

Below: the bathroom of today has everything for sanitation and convenience. In this one, the wash basins can be adjusted up or down to suit the height of whoever is using it.

Machines to Work

For hundreds of years, the burden of housework could be lightened only by servants. The technical advances of the Industrial Revolution made machines the helpers.

Right: an early version of a washing machine and wringer meant to make laundry days easier on milady, advertised in 1869.

Below: the sewing machine not only made mass production of clothing possible, but also made home sewing fun—even for a child.

Below right: the earliest Hoover vacuum cleaners appeared in the decade before World War I, and their popularity increased fast.

Right: it was heavy, it was cumbersome, but the flat iron of Victorian days was still an advance over the earlier types of irons.

Above center: the home cook who wanted the most modern stove in Victorian England would probably choose this heavy iron one.

Above right: does she think the robot would make a good playmate? People once thought that robots might make good maids.

Right: a whole kitchen on a post—and all the latest labor-saving devices are included.

The Car and You

Nothing has changed life so much as the introduction and use of the automobile. In fact, the car is almost a way of life in America—especially in the many sprawling suburbs.

Right: a lady didn't drive when cars were new—she was to be driven by a chauffeur.

Below: the big breakthrough for women drivers came in World War I, when many females drove as part of the war effort.

Below left: not long after World War I, gas companies began directing their ads to women drivers to sell more of their product.

Below right: though old, this cartoon on women drivers from an English magazine shows an atitude of ridicule that lingers on.

Buy Shell Oil this way—

DOUBLE SHELL MOTOR OIL

No Waste-No Mess

'And do I have to keep on holding this?'

Below: women drivers have proved to be not only as capable as men, but also as daring. Shown here is a female car racing competitor.

Above: today's woman depends on the car as a part of modern life—and enjoys it most for the freedom of action it can bring her.

Jacquie Bond-Smith

The Competent Woman

Is there anything a woman can't do today? She's a doctor, an engineer, an architect, a scientist—even an astronaut. Our female forebears could only dream of making achievements outside the home—but we do it.

Above: traditionally and for a long time, the kitchen, housework, and child rearing were women's primary fields of competence.

Below: said in jest or not, there is still social pressure on girls and boys to fill given roles in traditional ways, but it lessens all the time.

Boys invent things.   Girls use what boys invent.

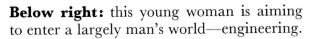

Above and below: more and more women are doing things once called "man's work". These are classes in carpentry and welding.

Below right: this young woman is aiming to enter a largely man's world—engineering.

Above: one of the few at the top in her field, this woman directs work on guided missiles.

You Can Fix It!

1

You may be a queen holding sway in a fairy tale castle, with scads of servants and an inexhaustible royal purse. Or you may be a multimillionairess living in a brand-new house that's kept in perfect condition by an army of unseen hired help. If you are like most of us, however, and fit into neither category, there are probably at least half-a-dozen things around your house or apartment that need fixing right now, and an equal number you would give almost anything to have improved.

Some of the jobs that need doing may simply be to eliminate a minor annoyance. Some, however, may be dangerous if left unrepaired. Maybe the toilet growls and gurgles, and requires a special wrist action to make it stop running after you have flushed it. That is annoying. But if your favorite reading lamp flicks on and off in an unpredictable and infuriating way, that is both annoying and dangerous. Such a lamp could easily cause a fire.

Perhaps your problem is a bedroom window that won't open without a struggle, or a door which lets in such a gale that, instead of spending your evenings comfortably relaxed in a housecoat or robe, you have to bundle yourself up like a female Dan McGrew in sweaters, scarves, and sweat-socks.

Try as you will, however, you can't get any of these small jobs taken care of either

Everyday of your life you use tools and machines much more complicated than any of the simple tools required for most of the fixit jobs explained in this book. If you can follow a pattern, measure, cut to size, and operate your sewing machine, you have already mastered the basic handyman skills.

by husband, friend, or repairman. If that's the case, you may find yourself thinking, "Well, I'll fix it myself." Then, just as soon as that thought pops into your mind, you will probably reply that "I really don't know how."

This mental exchange does not have to end with your giving up at the start. You can take it on faith that you can fix it if you try. The reason you can be so confident is that, if you watch most men tackle a fixit job, you'll soon develop a sneaking suspicion that the average man really doesn't know much about repairs either. Simply out of pride, or masculine bullheadedness, however, the average man will just go ahead, rushing in where angels fear to tread, and crash and bang about making a big mess. In doing so he will keep watching, looking, studying, and—some of the time—discovering what is wrong and making the necessary repairs. So there isn't any secret to doing repairs around the house, nor are men inherently any better at it than women. Most women I know can do a fixit job with much less fussing, and with at least 90 per cent less groaning and cursing. Almost any woman can do any household fixit job that can be safely handled by any home handyman.

Don't think that it's always easy, or that you will get perfect results the first time. Did your first apple pie turn out perfectly—or your first attempt at making a skirt? Probably not perfect, but probably not too bad. In just the same way, then—not perfectly, perhaps, but acceptably—you can fix that gurgling toilet, repair a leaky faucet, take the flicker out of your lamp, and do something about the drafts. More often than

The Fixit Rules

The three fixit Rules apply to any home repair problem. Rule 1 tells you to look and look again before you leap. Rule 2 says that things are not always what they seem, because any appliance or object is a system of parts, and time and wear alter the way they fit and work. Rule 3 is cautionary: the idea is to keep your cool; if you lose your temper, you may fluff the whole job.

Rule 1. Everything works in a logical way, so look at the job and think before you start.

not, you will spend a few cents, or a dollar or two, and some of your time to do a job that would cost anywhere from $8 for a plumber's call to $50, $60, or more—and often with no guarantee of when it will get done.

This book is your book of recipes for household repairs. Before we get to details, however, I'd like to share with you some general ideas I've learned in my years of hammering and banging. I think I've discovered three unshakable and unfailing principles that any woman can use to free herself from the tyranny of things that won't work, and the sometimes annoying traits of the men who rather condescendingly—and often expensively and far too slowly—get around to fixing them for us.

Rule 1. *Everything works in a logical way, so look at the job and think before you start.*

The only reasonable way to begin most jobs is by saying to yourself, "when this was working the way it should, it did thus and so in such and such an order." (By the way, you may find that talking to yourself helps.) Then look, and push, and poke a little bit here and there. Soon you will discover how the whatever-it-is is supposed to work, and

why it isn't now. When you have discovered where the trouble is, then some idea of what to do to put it right will begin to take shape in your mind.

I also learned that when I have to take something apart, it is best to lay aside the pieces in order, just the way they come off. Dump them in a pile like the children's dirty socks in the hamper, and you will find that getting them in the right order again is much harder than sorting out socks.

Rule 1 also means that you shouldn't force things into place. If the parts don't slip in smoothly, or go into place with just a little push, then something is wrong. It won't be put right with a good smack of the hammer. Start over again, and hunt for the logic. Fixing takes brain, not brawn. Now we come to Rule 2.

Rule 2. *Part A never fits Part B exactly—or almost never.*

If you have ever tried to assemble an inexpensive table that came in a flat package, or put a doll house together after the kids have gone to bed on Christmas eve, you know what I mean. Sometimes the instructions seem to have been written by a Greek

18

Rule 2. Part A never fits Part B exactly—or almost never.

Rule 3. Don't lose your temper, or everything will go wrong.

schoolboy in his first semester of English. Sometimes they don't even tell you where Part B goes. All too often, Part B isn't there, or it doesn't look like the picture in the instructions.

Rule 2 is not meant to discourage you, but to give you the real truth about home repairs. Doing your own home repairs is a bit like making a suit from a paper pattern. You usually have to put a little of your own alteration on it, because, if you are like the author of this book—that is, with Part A being a size 8, but with Part B closer to size 10—the pattern needs a little help. Exactly the same principle holds 'for books like this one. Every fixit project we've written about works. Most of them have been done by the author, and the rest have been checked and rechecked by experts. But the instructions are general. Chances are that your faucets don't look like the ones in the illustrations. Nevertheless, the principle is the same.

The fixit recipes in this book will help you to success if you remember that the Parts A and B in your house are probably just a little bit different from those in the pictures. Don't despair, because you can fix it—if you try.

Rule 3. *Don't lose your temper, or everything will go wrong.*

This rule comes into play when the first two don't produce results—when your attempts to diagnose the problem won't provide an answer, or when you know exactly what needs to be done, but nothing fits as it should. It really means that the faucet that continues to go drip, drip, drip in the night with exactly the same effect as Chinese water torture, even after your efforts to repair it, isn't trying to drive you crazy. The pesky thing is just an inanimate object of bits of metal that needs more work to make it work. So don't attack it in anger, or with revenge in mind, sweet as the thought may be. The rule is, "take it easy, lady."

Doors that stick and switches that won't produce light are inert, senseless objects. Getting them to operate properly requires a cool head, but no force. Any time you find yourself saying, "I'll get even with you, you nasty so-and-so", the job is sure to go wrong. Personally, I've found it a good idea not to start any complicated job, such as papering a wall, or laying bathroom tiles on a day I am feeling in the least cranky.

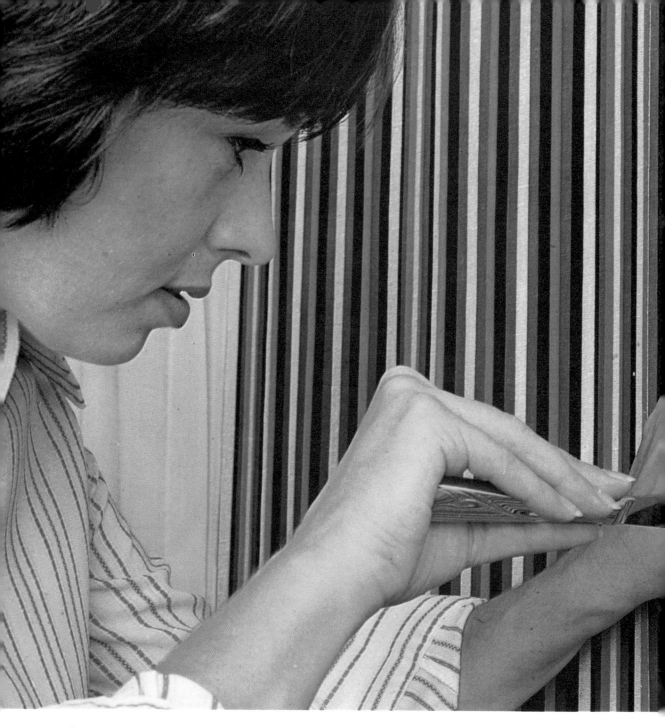

Tools for Ms. Fixit
2

If either of the above scenes looks like you, it's time to invest in a few proper tools—at least a good screwdriver and hammer. While it's possible to put up a towel rack with a knife, and hang a picture with a shoe, the results will be better if the tools are right.

A few common tools—a good hammer, an adjustable wrench, a screwdriver or two—are just as essential for setting up housekeeping as a set of pots and pans, sharp kitchen knives, and a can opener.

To simplify things and spare your budget, divide your basic tool list into three stages.

Stage 1. *The Handywoman's Home Survival Kit* represents something under $10 worth of tools that every household must not be without. It is an emergency kit that will get through any number of repair troubles.

Stage 2. *The Fixit Kit* consists of tools that, when added bit by bit to your tool chest, will put you in the way of handling 90 per cent of all the home repairs that can safely be done by amateurs—either men or women.

Stage 3. *Luxuries and Handy Nonessentials* are tools that you don't really need, such as an electric drill, electric sander, and stapler.

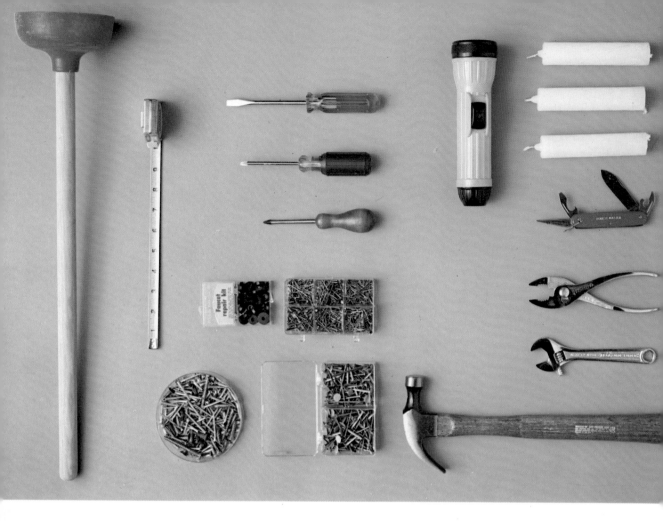

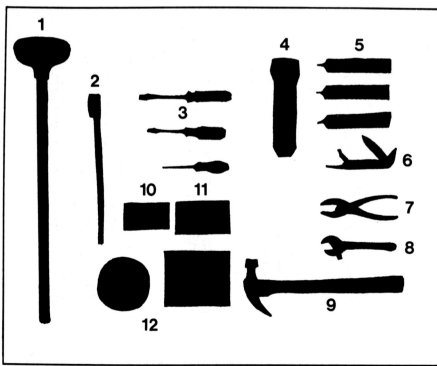

Stage 1 Survival Kit

Plumber's helper (1) clears stopped and sluggish drains. Steel tape (2) is the basic measuring tool. Screwdriver, Phillips screwdriver, and hand auger (3) for regular screws, Phillips screws, and making pilot holes. Flashlight (4) and candles (5) are essential for electrical emergencies. A good Scout or Swiss army knife (6) has a hundred uses. All-purpose pliers (7) or crescent wrench (8) will handle most nut-and-bolt problems. Curved claw hammer (9) is important; should weigh 16 ounces. Washers, screws, and nails (10-12) finish the kit.

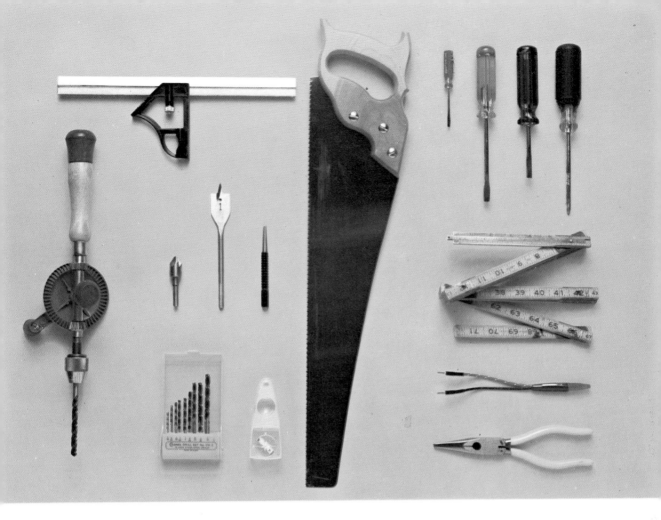

Stage 2 Fixit Kit

A good quality hand drill (1) with a set of fractional bits (2) is versatile. Countersink (3) and spade bit (4) will help in drilling operations. Nail set (5) for neat finishing. Use combination square (6) to measure and mark boards to cut with crosscut saw (7). Screwdrivers of different lengths and tip sizes (8) are always useful. Wooden rule (9) is flexible, convenient. Circuit tester (10) helps prevent shocks, and electrician's pliers (11) are one of the handiest items for electrical repairs. Stud finder (12) is useful in putting up shelves.

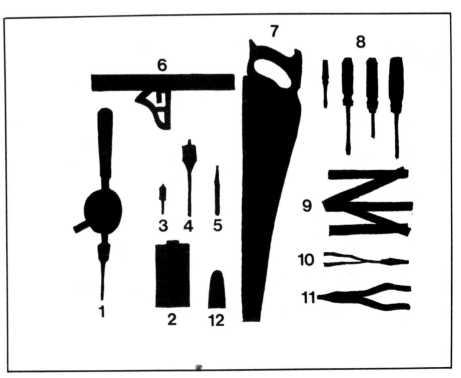

That is, you don't need any of them until you first use one. Then you will find it so handy, you won't want to be without it.

Tips on Buying and Using Tools
Home repair experts often suggest that you buy tools only when you need them, but common sense says that if you follow that advice too literally, you could easily get stuck. Somehow emergencies always seem to occur on weekends and evenings, when the stores are closed.

Buy your tools at a hardware store or lumberyard sales office, and choose one with friendly, courteous, and patient clerks. You will want to ask questions, and compare prices. I suggest that you don't buy either the least or the most expensive. Tell the clerk what tools you have in mind, and he will

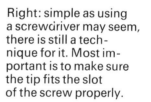

be able to help you make a suitable choice.

Tools for Fastening
Numerous home fixit jobs require that you fasten something, so the essential and most-used tools will be your hammer and screwdrivers. To the uninitiated eye all hammers look alike, but the one you want is a 16-ounce *curved claw* hammer with a flat face (the part that hits the nail.) It will be heavy enough for any job but building a house, and not so light that it will take you a million swings to drive a big nail easily.
Using Your Hammer. Whether driving nails or cracking hickory nuts—don't choke your hammer. Hold the handle near the end, and swing it with plenty of wrist action. In this

manner, the hammer head does the work.

I can't tell you how many times I hammered my left thumb and forefinger before I learned that, to start a nail, it should be held high under the head, and not down near the point. Then, if you miss, you will knock your fingers aside without too much damage, rather than smashing them.

Try to start the nails at a slight angle, because they will hold better. Once you have carefully started a nail with a few taps, pound it in with hard strokes. You will find that your square hit score will increase, and that you will bend fewer nails, if you keep your eye fixed on the nail head.

To pull a nail, wedge the V of the hammer claw around the nail's shank between the nailhead and the wood, and then rock the hammer backward. Guard against marring a

Left: the hand auger is useful for making pilot holes for small screws.

Right: simple as using a screwdriver may seem, there is still a technique for it. Most important is to make sure the tip fits the slot of the screw properly.

fine wood surface by placing a flat stick under the hammerhead. When pulling a balky nail, place a thicker piece of wood under the hammer for increased leverage.
Screwdrivers. Next to your hammer, the screwdrivers in your tool chest will be the instruments you reach for most often. For the Stage 1 Survival Kit buy two, with handles about six inches long. One of them should be a Phillips screwdriver. Its tip is shaped like an X, and fits the cross-slotted heads of the Phillips screws you find so often on cabinet and drapery hardware, appliances, and toys. Add others in different lengths and tip sizes as you go along. A screwdriver with the handle rather large in proportion to the shank gives you more leverage, and lets you

When starting a nail, hold it near the head. If you miss, you will only knock your fingers out of the way, rather than smash them between the board and hammer.

First give the nail a few taps, and then drive it in with full swings. Grip the hammer at the end of the handle. This way, your arm action will make the hammer's head do the hard work.

When pulling nails, a block of wood under the hammer's head gives leverage, and reduces effort. The block also prevents marring of the surface. If nails are hard to pull, work them from side to side with the claw of the hammer.

exert more force. A long screwdriver lets you apply more power than a shorter one with a tip of the same size.

Pliers. There are literally dozens of kinds of pliers, each designed for some special purpose. Only two types are necessary for the home repairwoman. The *all-purpose pliers* (Stage 1) and the *round-nosed electrician's pliers* (Stage 2).

The all-purpose pliers will handle most of the nut-and-bolt situations you are apt to run into. They have a peculiar double joint that allows them to work in two positions, the normal position, and the wide position to grasp large nuts. I also find use for this tool in the kitchen to open the screw caps of new ketchup bottles, and to pry off stuck caps of syrup bottles without having to call for a man to help. This versatile tool will also cut wire if you place the wire well back in its jaws. You may have to finish the cut with a few back and forth bends, but the operation is simple enough.

The electrician's pliers are not designed to grasp nuts, but to bend and cut wire. Not only are they invaluable in electrical work for cutting a wire, scraping off its insulation, and twisting it around the small screws called terminals, but the long tapered jaws can also act as extremely strong, fine fingers. You will find your electrician's pliers the ideal tool for holding tacks and small nails while you drive them, and also for pulling them out again.

Wrenches. If your fixit plans do not include plumbing repairs beyond replacing leaky faucet washers, you can get by with an *adjustable crescent wrench.* I suggest, however, that someday you also buy a *pipe wrench* (Stage 2). It will come in handy if you ever have to dismantle the trap under the bathroom sink to clean a stoppage, or retrieve a ring or watch. But if you plan to operate a one-wrench shop, buy a crescent wrench that opens to two-and-a-half or three inches. Here I might mention another luxury, the *lock wrench,* shown in the picture on page 27. Use it when you want to get a strong grip that absolutely will not slip.

Electrician's pliers are handy, and have many uses. One is to help you hold small nails and tacks in order to start them (above); another is to pull nails with heads too small for hammer's claws (below).

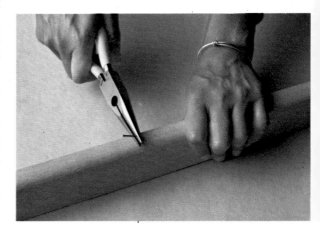

Saws and Sawing

Saws are really more for making it than fixing it. Of all your first fixit tools, it is likely to be the one you will use least of all. Nevertheless, when you need a saw there is no substitute. You can possibly use a knife as a screwdriver, but you cannot saw a board with a breadknife. So your Stage 2 tools should include a handsaw of the type known as a *crosscut saw.* It is used for straight cuts across the grain of all types of wood and wood panels. Crosscut saws are available with from 6 to 11 teeth (points) per inch. The most practical selection for the home handywoman is an 8-point saw with a 24-inch blade. It won't make as fine a cut as a 10- or 11-point saw, but it will cut faster and with less effort. Should you need it for *ripping* (cutting with the grain) as well, it

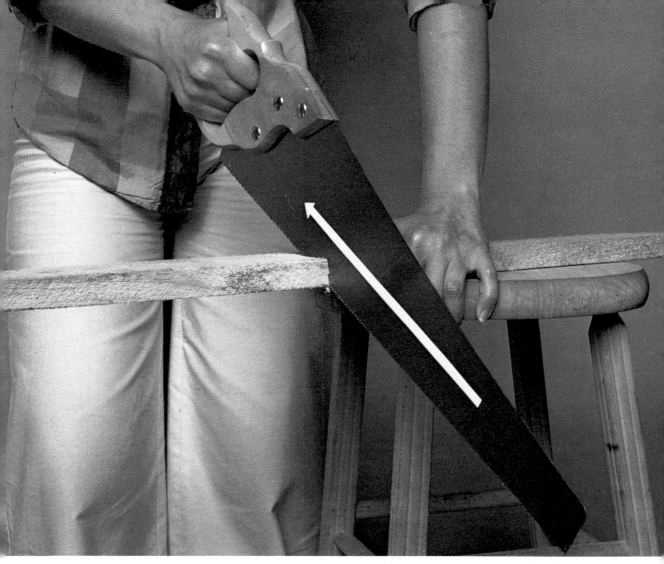

Left: a lock wrench is not essential, but it will become a favorite if you use it once. The jaw opening is adjusted by a knurled screw at the end of the handle.

Above: the job of sawing will be somewhat easier if you do these two things: saw on the waste end— that is, the outside—of the line you have drawn as a guide; hold your saw at a 45-degree angle to the work, and start the cut with short upward pulls.

Once the lock wrench is fitted and closed, it will not slip. It gives you a secure hold on pipes, rods, and bolts.

will do a fair job. But take a tip from an old fixit hand. If you have a number of boards to saw, have most of the cutting done by the friendly man in the lumberyard. This service is usually free. You had better be sure, however, that the measurements you specify are accurate, because boards don't stretch. But if you must saw at home, you will find cutting easiest if you hold the saw at an angle of 45 degrees to the surface. If you are right-handed, watch the cutting line from the left side of the blade. If you are left-handed, watch it from the right side. Always saw on the outside of your mark,

27

The combination square can be put to many uses. Above it serves as a T-square by which you can make sure your sawing guideline is straight.

Here the combination square is used to mark a miter cut. You draw the proper line by resting the angled part of the square against the edge of the board.

because you can always cut off a little more, but you cannot add on a single jot.

Start the cut with short strokes drawn upward, and then progress to smooth, full strokes. Prevent the wood's underside from breaking out as you cut by first scoring it with your jackknife. As you near the end of the cut, support the excess piece so that it won't break off.

If you have problems in keeping the cut straight, clamp a straight board along the cutting line for the side of the saw to ride against.

Tools for Drilling Holes

While you go around your home tightening up this and that, you are bound to discover six new places in which you want to screw something new into place. For the small screws on drapery hardware, cup hooks, and such, you can start the hole with your *hand auger*. Sooner or later, however, you are going to want to hang up something that calls for screws longer or wider than you can start with that handy tool. For this purpose you will need a good quality *hand drill* (Stage 2 tools). Buy a drill that will take bits up to $\frac{1}{4}$ inch. When you buy, ask the dealer for a drill that has *universal jaws*, because it

will take bits with both square and round shanks.

Two useful additions are a *spade bit* for drilling large holes, and a *countersink* for drilling cone-shaped holes so that you can set the heads of wood screws flush with the surface of your work.

The bits you will find most useful come in a set of seven, sized in 32nds of an inch (1/16, 3/32, $\frac{1}{8}$, 5/32, 3/16, 7/32, $\frac{1}{4}$), and all done up in a handy case.

The *electric drill* is the first luxury you should give a thought to. Even if you use it only a few times a year, you will soon find yourself completely devoted to this most versatile tool. If you can operate an electric mixer, you won't have any trouble with an electric drill. With it you can drill holes in metal and masonry as well as in wood. With attachments, your drill will also become a sander, polisher, and paint mixer.

Now, the confusing part about the kind of electric drill most useful for general household repair jobs is that it is called a $\frac{1}{4}$-inch drill, which has nothing to do with the size of the hole you're drilling. The $\frac{1}{4}$-inch name describes the nondrilling end of the bit, which you insert in the *chuck* (the part that holds the bits). The $\frac{1}{4}$-inch figure indicates

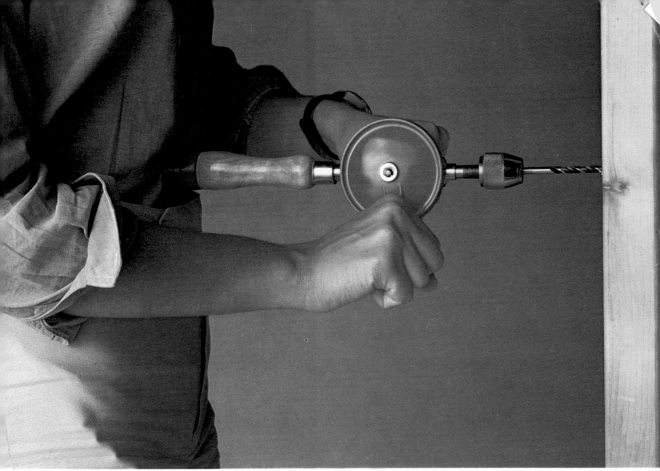

To keep a hand drill in a straight line while working horizontally, when both hands are on the handles, put a slight pressure on the tool with your stomach (above). When drilling vertically (right), hold the drill in place with one hand on the shank.

the maximum diameter this drill should handle.

Many drills and other portable electric tools come with three-pronged plugs on the cord. The third prong acts as a "ground", and guarantees a no-shock performance. If you don't have a three-hole outlet handy, you can buy a three-hole plug with a prong that fits into a two-hole outlet. The hanging wire on the plug goes behind the center screw of the outlet plate. Just loosen the screw slightly, slip the wire under, and tighten the screw again.

Measuring Tools

The handywoman's first measuring tool should be a flexible steel tape. We have put it in our kits as a Stage 1 survival tool. Then, when you can afford $2 or $3, invest in a

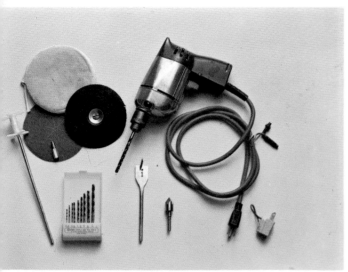

Above: the electric drill is a complete workshop in itself. This kit has disks for sanding and buffing, a paint stirrer, and special bits.

Left: use the key to fasten a bit into the drill chuck. It's a good idea to keep the key attached to the cord of the drill with a rubber band or twine.

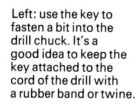

Right: when using the drill as a sander, remember that the cuts it makes will be circular. It is best for rough work, such as removing old finishes, and on the end grain.

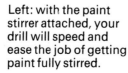

Left: with the paint stirrer attached, your drill will speed and ease the job of getting paint fully stirred.

folding wooden rule like the one shown in the Stage 2 photograph.

Start off with a 6- or 12-foot tape. If you buy one that recoils automatically, make sure there's some way to lock it in the extended position. The cases of good quality tapes are exactly two inches long—very handy when you want to make accurate measurements inside a window frame.

Because it is rigid when open, a folding wooden rule can be extended for some distance without support at the far end. Try

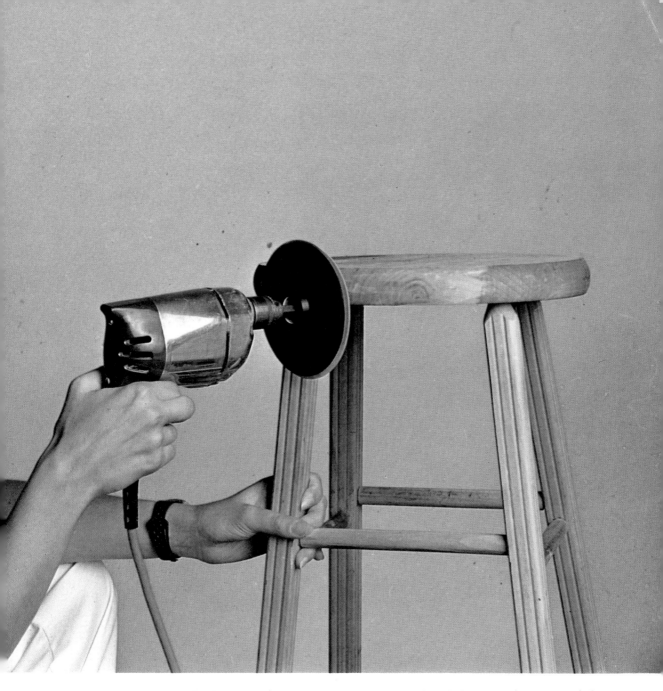

measuring a wide window all alone, and you will see how useful this feature is. At one end there is a sliding extension for precise inside measurements. Did you ever want to measure around a corner? Well, you can with the folding rule. Simply bend it around the corner.

The *combination square* is shown in the Stage 2 picture. It looks like a baroque musical instrument without its strings. Very handy it is, for like your electric drill, it has many uses. You can use it as a square to see

whether the ends of the boards are straight, or to cut a straight line; as a miter gauge to make accurate cuts at an angle; and as a level and 12-inch rule. The tool's freely sliding 12-inch handle can be tightened to the blade, or removed. Because the handle meets the blade at a 45-degree angle on one side, and a 90-degree angle on the other, the tool will check for precise 45-degree miter as well as for square. Most combination squares are equipped with a spirit level for checking true level and plumb (that is, a true vertical.)

Fascinating Fasteners
3

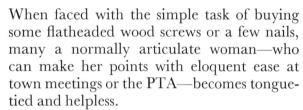

When you use the right tools and the right fasteners for the job, you will come up with a finished product you can be proud of—one that is useful, long lasting, and attractive.

When faced with the simple task of buying some flatheaded wood screws or a few nails, many a normally articulate woman—who can make her points with eloquent ease at town meetings or the PTA—becomes tongue-tied and helpless.

If you are going to take doing your own repairs seriously, my advice is that you learn the right name for things. A speaking knowledge of the fixit language will enable you to buy exactly what you want and need, and save time, money, and embarrassment.

Since most of your handywoman tasks will involve fastening things to other things, hanging objects on walls, and sticking this to that, this chapter deals with fasteners of various kinds, and methods for using them.

Nails and How to Choose Them
There are nails for every purpose. The kinds that you will use most often, however, are *common nails* and *finishing nails*. The common nail is just what its name implies: it is the ordinary, everyday, flatheaded nail with a diamond-shaped point.

When the appearance of flat nailheads on the surface of your finished project would prove unsightly, use small-headed nails. They can be easily punched down below the surface of the wood with your nail set. (See Stage 2 tools.) This leaves small holes, which can then be filled with putty or plastic wood. You will want to use finishing nails for putting up moldings and trim, as well as for repairs to cabinets, and some kinds of furniture. Very small finishing nails, measuring from $\frac{1}{2}$ to $1\frac{1}{2}$ inches in length, are referred to as brads. They are useful for fine work in which little or no stress is involved.

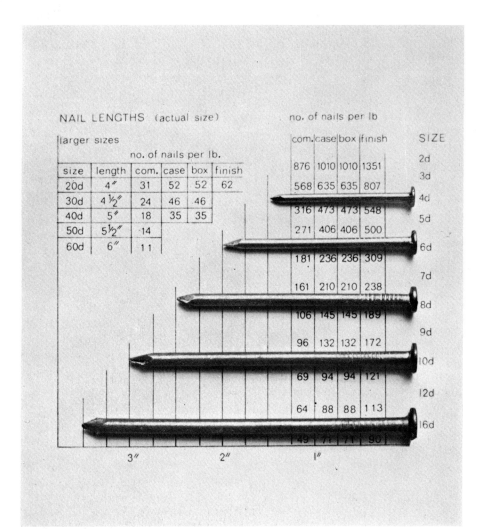

NAIL LENGTHS (actual size)   no. of nails per lb

larger sizes

		no. of nails per lb.			
size	length	com.	case	box	finish
20d	4"	31	52	52	62
30d	4½"	24	46	46	
40d	5"	18	35	35	
50d	5½"	14			
60d	6"	11			

com.	case	box	finish	SIZE
876	1010	1010	1351	2d
568	635	635	807	3d
				4d
316	473	473	548	5d
271	406	406	500	6d
181	236	236	309	7d
161	210	210	238	8d
106	145	145	189	9d
96	132	132	172	10d
69	94	94	121	12d
64	88	88	113	16d
49	71	71	90	

3"   2"   1"

Nail sizes are expressed as "penny", abbreviated as "d". This chart shows common, box, and finishing nails in 4d, 6d, 8d, 12d, and 16d sizes. Use this guide to select nails of the right size for the job at hand. Remember, it's cheaper to buy nails loose by the pound than in packages of various small sizes.

Using Nails

Obviously, the larger the nail, the greater the holding power; but large nails are more likely to split the wood. To minimize the frustration of splitting a piece of wood, always select the smallest nail that will give you the results shown in the diagram on page 35. If you are remodeling an old house or apartment, or restoring an old cabinet in which the wood is apt to be very dry, or if you are working with very hard wood, drill small holes—called pilot holes—in which to start the nails. Another trick I learned from an old-time carpenter that will also minimize the danger of splitting is to blunt the point first by hammering on it while holding the nail upside down. Although I can't tell you why, blunt nails are less likely to split the wood when driven in near the edge, and they actually hold better. When the job calls for several nails to be driven at close intervals, don't drive them along the same streak of grain. Stagger them instead.

Wood Screws

Screws not only hold better than nails in wood, but, when properly set, can also draw pieces together to make a stronger, neater union than you can achieve with nails. Whenever you want your work to hold up for a long period under hard use, or in places subject to strain, screws are the fasteners of choice—for example, putting up shelves, drapery hardware, and hinges of all types.

The trouble with screws, however, is that, although the threads are sharp enough to make nasty scratches on furniture, and even to give you a painful cut, they aren't sharp

For fine carpentry, you won't want unsightly nail-heads on the surface of your work. In this case, use finishing nails, and countersink (drive the heads below the surface) with a tool called a nail set.

You will find that you are much less likely to split boards when nailing them if you blunt the tip of the nail by hammering on it. This also gives greater holding power. A few gentle taps will be enough.

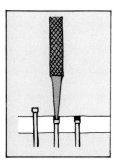

Left: a diagram showing how to countersink nailheads. Step one is to drive the nail in until the head remains slightly above surface. Then put the nail set on the head squarely, and drive it below the surface a bit. Finally fill the hole with wood filler, and sand the surface smooth.
Below: helpful tips in nail use.

enough to drill their way through anything but the softest of wood. So, driving a screw is always a two-step process. First, you must make a pilot hole for the screw, then you sink it into place. For short screws of up to a half-inch in length—the kind you'll use for shade fixtures, towel racks, and other hardware of this kind—use your hand awl. Be

1. Nails should be 2½ to 3 times longer than thickness of board they will be nailed into.

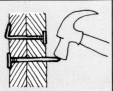

2. Nails driven through opposite side and clinched (bent into wood) gives much strength.

3. Toenailed joints can be set in if you angle nails as shown.

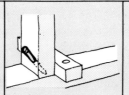

4. To start first toenail, use block tacked in place to steady upright piece.

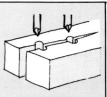

5. Nails driven into same streak of grain may split the wood. Blunt ends of nails and stagger.

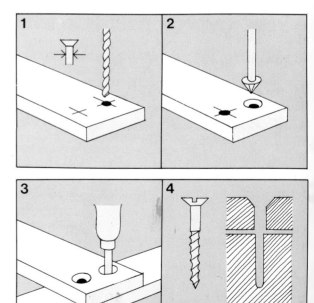

WOOD SCREW SIZES . . . Shortest length in each gauge shown as actual size, other lengths indicated by arrow points.

Gauge numbers: 14 12 11 10 9 8 7 6 5 4 3 2

Length scale (right side): ¼" ½" ¾" 1" 1½" 2" 2½" 3"

LARGER SIZES — Shank diam. actual size.

16	18	22	24
1¼"-3"	1½"-4"	1¾"-4"	3½"-4"

Left: use this chart to choose screws so that at least ⅔—and never less than ½—of their length can be driven into the surface you are working on. When fastening boards, select screw ⅛ inch shorter than the combined thickness of the boards so that there is no danger the screw will protrude.

Below: to countersink screw, first locate and mark its position, and drill hole large enough so that screw passes without binding. Second, use countersink tool to drill another hole that matches the diameter of the screw head. Third, place pieces together in position, and use a hand auger to mark a pilot hole. Fourth, drill a pilot hole in which you'll start the threaded end of the screw.

sure that you center it on the spot you want the screw to go in, and hold it vertically to the surface. Press down hard, and turn the awl to make a hole just deep enough for you to turn the screw in by hand until it stays in place. Then it is no trick at all to finish the job with a screwdriver.

Longer screws—up to an inch or so in length—require pilot holes drilled to the full length of the screw. Be careful that the bit you use is no larger in diameter than the shaft of the threaded end of the screw—that is, not larger than the solid part between the threads. Should you make a mistake, and drill the pilot so large that the threads won't bite and hold, you can repair the damage. With your jackknife, whittle a peg to fit the useless hole, soak it with glue, and tap it into place. Cut off the peg flush with the surface,

These directions for putting up a towel rack will apply in any case in which you are fastening something to wood paneling. It's an easy job.

and then redrill the proper size pilot hole.

Big screws—long ones, or those large in diameter—will go in easier if you drill the pilot in two steps:
1. Drill the first hole of correct size to the depth the screw will reach as described above.
2. Drill a second, larger hole to the depth and diameter of the shank, or smooth part under the head, but not a bit deeper.

This double drill routine still gives you full holding power, but saves the trouble of exerting force to drive the long unthreaded part of the screw through the narrow pilot hole. No matter what size screws you work with, you'll find they always go in easier if you rub the threads across a cake of soap before you begin to drive them into place. Any soap will do, but I prefer old-fashioned yellow laundry soap.

There is one other thing you should know about screws. Unlike nails, their heads cannot set flush to the surface of the work unless you drill out the top of the pilot hole to fit the conical shaped head. This operation—shown in the photos on page 35—is performed with a special bit known as a countersink (see Stage 2 tools). This tool, costing less than $1, is essential for neatly finished work in which screws are used.

Above: place towel rack in the position you want it, and mark the location of the screws by pencil. Below: use a hand auger to make pilot holes, and drill them just deep enough to accept tip of screw.

Hollow Wall Fasteners

Sooner or later you are going to want to hang a mirror or painting, or put up some new shelves on an inside wall. Though your first impulse may be to get out your hammer and drive in some nails, this rarely works—at least not for long. Since interior walls are usually hollow, the nail merely breaks into empty space, and it won't be long before your new shelves come down with a bang, leaving you with some cracked plaster, and an ugly useless hole. Don't despair, because no matter what size or weight of the fixture you want to hang, there is a fastener available for the job. For small pictures, decora-

Above: match holes of rack to pilot holes and drive the first screw snugly but not tightly. Realign the rack, and drive another screw at the opposite end. Make these two tight, then drive others.

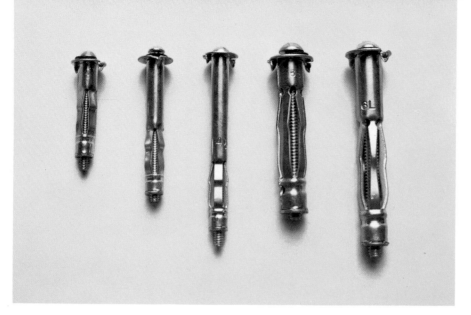

The most versatile and easiest to use of hollow wall fasteners are Molly bolts. They are available in many sizes for use in walls of different thicknesses, and with things of varying weight. The complete bolt is passed through the pilot hole. When its screw is tightened, the bolt expands behind the wall, as shown in the photograph at right.

tive plates, and racks for your collection of silver coffee spoons, there are adhesive backed hangers which can be cemented in place against the wall. Use caution, however, because this type of device sticks to the surface only; its holding power is limited by the strength of the surface (paint or wallpaper) already in place on the wall. If the fixture comes down, you are likely to lose some paint or paper along with it.

Small mirrors, decorative shelves, and framed paintings up to 40 pounds or so can be hung safely and securely with special picture hooks designed to hold the nail at a proper angle to give strong holding power in either plaster or wallboard. Before you hammer one of these fasteners in place, stick a wide strip of cellulose tape over the spot where the nail will enter to prevent cracking the plaster.

For maximum holding strength in all types of hollow walls, you must use fasteners with expanding wings or ribs, which open up behind the wall when a bolt or screw is tightened in the center.

Expansion-type screws—most often known by the trade name Molly bolt, although many of them aren't—consist of a tube or sleeve which is inserted into a hole drilled through the wall. When the screw inside the sleeve is tightened, the sleeve spreads out behind the wall. They have an advantage over most hollow wall fasteners in that the

bolt can be removed whenever necessary, while the sleeve remains anchored in its original position in the wall. This enables you to take down fixtures and to replace them simply by unscrewing the bolt whenever the mood strikes. Very short ones are available for such jobs as hanging mirrors or other appliances on hollow-core flush doors, as well as for fastening to thin plywood and composition board.

Masonry Fasteners

When you are faced with an irresistible yen to fasten shelves, cabinets, or other fixtures to solid masonry walls in basements or on the outside of the house, there are a number of different fastening devices that you can use. But, unless you feel life will be incomplete without that whatever screwed tightly to that brick or concrete wall, forget it, or call a handyman. This is one job that is far easier in the telling than in the doing. If, however, domestic tranquility and fulfilled womanhood depends upon it, the fasteners you need are expansion type anchors. They are usually made of lead, or a special heavy-duty fiber. The anchors start at about $\frac{1}{8}$ inch in diameter, and are designed to take standard machine screws.

For light-duty jobs in which the stress is parallel to the surface—that is, down rather than straight out—use plastic anchors designed to hold wood screws. They are

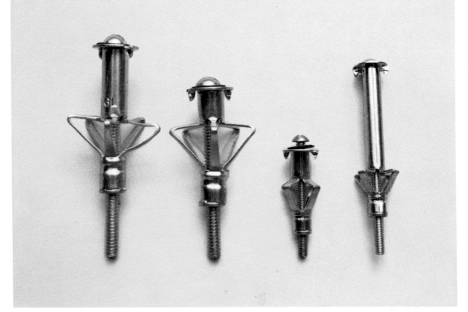

particularly suitable for use in brick walls for such jobs as hanging fireplace tools on a mantel, hanging pictures or mirrors, and fastening shutters on brick or stucco.

Now the work begins, because you have to drill a hole of the proper size in the masonry wall to accept the anchor. Then, the proper screw or bolt is inserted, the shield or anchor expands inside its hole to lock itself firmly—

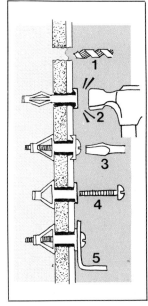

To install Molly bolts, drill a pilot hole just large enough for the bolt to pass, and tap lightly to fix flanges to wall. Then turn the screw to expand the wings, and anchor the bolt. Withdraw the screw, and attach what you are fastening. Re-insert and tighten screw.

When you want to fasten something, don't overlook cements of various kinds. Two-part epoxy cements make permanent, nearly unbreakable bonds between different materials. Metal gluing mixtures seal holes in pipes, radiators, etc. Contact glue is excellent for furniture repairs when clamping is not practical. Plastic rubber and silicone cements provide flexible, and waterproof, seals.

and permanently—in place. To hold their positions in the holes before the bolts are inserted, most expansion anchors must be "set" by rapping with a hammer and punch.

To drill the required holes in a masonry wall, you can use either a star drill or a carbide-tipped masonry drill bit for a $\frac{1}{4}$-inch electric drill. Star drills are driven in with a heavy (two pound) hammer. It is no job for

Left: one type of masonry wall fastener consists of plastic anchor sleeves and screws. Use them when the load they will carry is moderate. Right: the first step in installing masonry fasteners is to mark the screw holes by scoring the masonry with a hard tool.

a lady. I recommend using the carbide-tipped bit with an ordinary electric drill, which you can always rent if you don't own one. Bits up to $\frac{1}{2}$ inch in diameter, with $\frac{1}{4}$-inch shanks to fit the chuck of your standard $\frac{1}{4}$-inch drill, can be purchased for a dollar or so. Wear protective glasses, make sure the drill is well grounded, and away you go. Bear down hard with steady pressure so that the bit cannot slip inside its hole. Slipping will cause it to dull rapidly.

I will admit that this job is just as hard as it sounds. Yet, if you follow the instructions for the type of anchor you choose, and work carefully and deliberately, you will succeed.

The Easy Way With Shelves

I don't know how the situation is in your house, but if it's like that in most American homes, you probably find yourself in a state of continual shelf crisis. No sooner have you installed some new ones, than someone buys more books or records, one of the children will take up a new hobby that calls for storage space, or you get the feeling there is too much junk lying around here and there, and more shelves are the answer.

These days there's no reason not to have all the shelving you want, where you want

it, and almost when you want it. Happily, by using one of the many varieties of patented screw-on shelf standards and brackets, you can easily install shelves yourself. Yet, I've known women who have had shelving installed by carpenters or handymen who charge at least $5 or $6 an hour, plus the cost of the materials.

If you have mastered the rudiments of

drilling holes and driving screws, you can do your shelving just as well yourself—and you don't have to hang around the house waiting endlessly for the carpenter to come. Let's call the slotted pieces that go on the wall *shelf standards*. The arms that hold the shelves we will call *brackets*.

Planning The Job

Before you go out to buy materials you have to determine the following:

1. *Spacing and Width of Shelves.* In any kind of shelf storage system, the idea is not to cram as many items as possible in a given shelf area, but to have enough shelves available to spread out the stored items so they can be seen, and are easily accessible. Eight-inch-wide shelves are satisfactory for most books, although 10-inch shelves give a better appearance. For other items, use the narrowest shelf that will meet the storage need. This way, items on the shelves don't get buried behind other items, and the weight is distributed more evenly over the wall area. The shelves can be an inch or two wider than the shelf brackets. Just drill a $\frac{1}{4}$-inch hole in the underside of the shelf to receive the tip of the shelf bracket. Depending on the look you want to achieve, the ends of the

Left: drill holes for plastic masonry anchors with special bit on the electric drill, and wear protective glasses. You must bear down hard, so should stand closer, and at a better angle, than the woman as pictured. Below: drill holes deep enough for whole anchor, and tap it into place.

Above: place hanger over anchors, insert and drive first screw snugly but not tightly. Realign hanger, and insert and tighten remaining screws. Right: the planter you wanted just where you wanted it—that's your reward for the not-so-easy job of fastening the hanger it needed to masonry.

shelves can extend from two to six inches beyond the brackets.

2. *Spacing of Shelf Standards.* The heavier the load you want to put on your shelf system, the closer you must space the shelf standards. If you're only going to make a decorative display of small items and a few books, you can space the standards from 32 to 36 inches apart. If you intend to keep heavy items on the shelves, such as large numbers of books, cans of paint, or canned goods, standards should be no more than 24 inches apart.

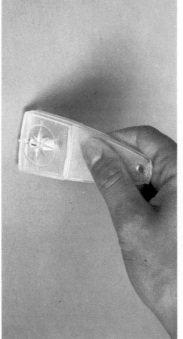
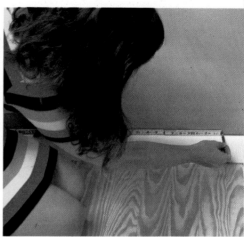

Left: a stud finder makes locating studs easier. It is simply a magnet that reacts to the nails holding wallboard to studs.

Below: studs are placed on 16-inch centers. After locating them, check spacing by drilling fine holes just above the molding.

Most inside walls are hollow, so shelves attached to them won't be able to carry much weight if you use hollow-wall fasteners. This means you should fasten your shelf standards to the wall studs. The simplest way to locate these is by pounding the wall with your fist (above). When you hear a dull, solid sound, the stud is probably there.

Below: typical hollow wall of wallboard or plaster over framing is built by nailing wallboard (1) to vertical studs (2). Double studs (3) at openings are called trimmer studs. Header (4) caps openings. Shelves on such walls should be fastened to studs with wood screws. Using hollow wall fasteners will work, but only for light loads.

3. *Shelf Materials.* You can have shelves cut to size from hardwood or fir plywood, or you can buy lumber and cut them yourself. Cover plywood edges with veneer edging tape, or thin strips of solid wood. Plywood is more resistant to sag and warp than solid wood, but solid wood is a good choice for utility shelves, or other applications in which appearance is not so important. An inexpensive grade of solid lumber is less costly than plywood, and requires no edge treatment. You can also buy ready-made shelves in kits, along with their correct hardware. While they have the advantage of being cut to size and nicely finished, precut shelves cost from two to three times more than plywood or lumber.

After you have carefully figured out how many lengths of shelf standard, how many brackets, and how many feet of shelving are required to finish the job, you are ready to shop around. By comparing prices, you can probably save yourself a worthwhile sum of money. Also, since you know what you need,

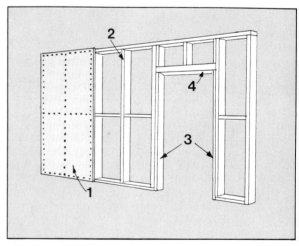

you can buy the full supply all at one time.

Putting Your Shelves Up
1. *How to Fasten Shelf Standards to Solid Wood Paneling.* You just screw the standards to the wall wherever you want them, using the screws provided. Drill holes for the screws, and rub a little soap or beeswax on the screw threads to make them easier to drive.

This type of installation will support any reasonable load. Your only concern is to space the standards close enough so the shelves won't sag.

2. *Fastening to Plaster or Wallboard.* You have two choices in this case. One is to locate the two-by-four studs under the wall surface, and mount the standards with screws through the wall surface into the studs. Most studs are spaced at 16 inches from center to center, so your standards will be spaced either 16 or 32 inches apart. Thirty-two inch spacing is satisfactory for most loads.

Locate studs by looking along the baseboard to see where it is nailed, by tapping the wall lightly with a hammer to find where it sounds most "solid," or by using a magnetic stud finder. If all else fails, you can drill a number of test holes to locate one stud,

What you have learned about fastening anything to a wall is all you really need to know in order to put up all your own home shelving—plain or fancy. Right: start by marking the spot for the top screw hole Below: make a pilot hole with an electric drill that is fitted with a small wood bit. Stand on something firm if so necessary to get into the right drilling position.

Below: drive in the top screw after rubbing it with soap or beeswax. Do not tighten this screw, so that the standard will plumb itself vertically.

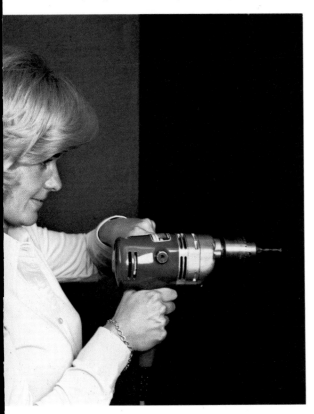

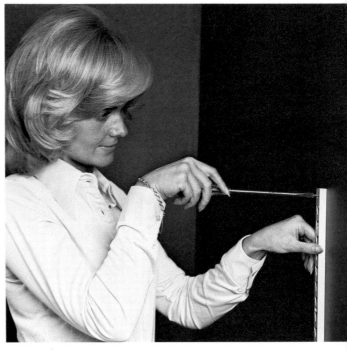

measure at 16-inch intervals to find others.

Usually the studs won't be where you want them, so you will have to use the other choice of hollow wall fasteners. If you find yourself in this situation, follow the instructions for hollow wall fasteners in the preceding pages. Before buying the fasteners, however, check the thickness of your wall with exploratory drill holes, and make sure that the center bolt is long enough.

3. *When You Have ¼-inch Plywood or Hardwood Paneling.* You can use either of the support systems described above for plaster or wallboard walls for ¼-inch paneling materials. Paneling is usually nailed either directly to studs, or to wood furring strips spaced on two foot centers. The studs or furring strips are easy to locate—just look in the grooves of the paneling to find where it is nailed. You can also use special short Molly bolts on paneling if your standard spacing doesn't correspond with furring strip placement. Either system works well. For narrow shelves, on which you plan to put only lightweight items, you can screw the standards directly to the paneling without locating studs or furring; but the load limit on such shelves should be kept to 10 to 15 pounds per foot.

4. *For Brick, Concrete Block, or Concrete Walls.* Follow the technique for solid wall fasteners

Above: align the standard with a carpenter's level, then mark and drill screw holes, and drive screws.

Below: measure off the space to the next standard; distance depends on the load to be carried.

Below right: after checking alignment by measuring from each base to floor, all screws are driven.

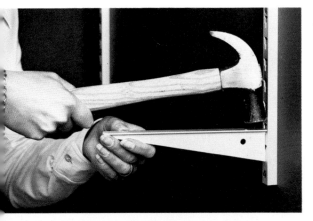

Left: to make a shelf bracket set properly and also fit firmly, tap it lightly but firmly with a hammer at its base.

on pages 38-40. Before you drill, however, consider mounting one-by-two inch wood strips to the masonry wall with epoxy cement. It will work very well. Let the glue dry for 48 hours, then simply screw the standards to the strips with wood screws.

5. *How to Align Shelf Standards*. Determine the correct distance from the floor to the top of the first standard, mark the top hole position, and drill for the first screw or other fastener. Fasten the standard by the top screw, leaving the screw loose enough so the standard will plumb itself vertically. If you have a carpenter's level, use it to plumb the standard. Now mark the other screw holes, swing the standard to one side, and drill. Align the tops of other standards with the first by using a carpenter's level, or a chalk line. If neither is available, measure the distance from the floor to the top of the last standard in line, then draw a line between the top of the first and last standards, using a board as a straight edge. Align the tops of intermediate standards with this line. If any standards are planned to extend to different heights, level them from the top of a corresponding slot in the first standard.

Above: add the shelves of your choice. These are eight inches wide, and three feet long.

Right: with your useful new shelves arranged in an attractive way—partly for use, and partly for show—you can surely smile in delight at a fixit job well done.

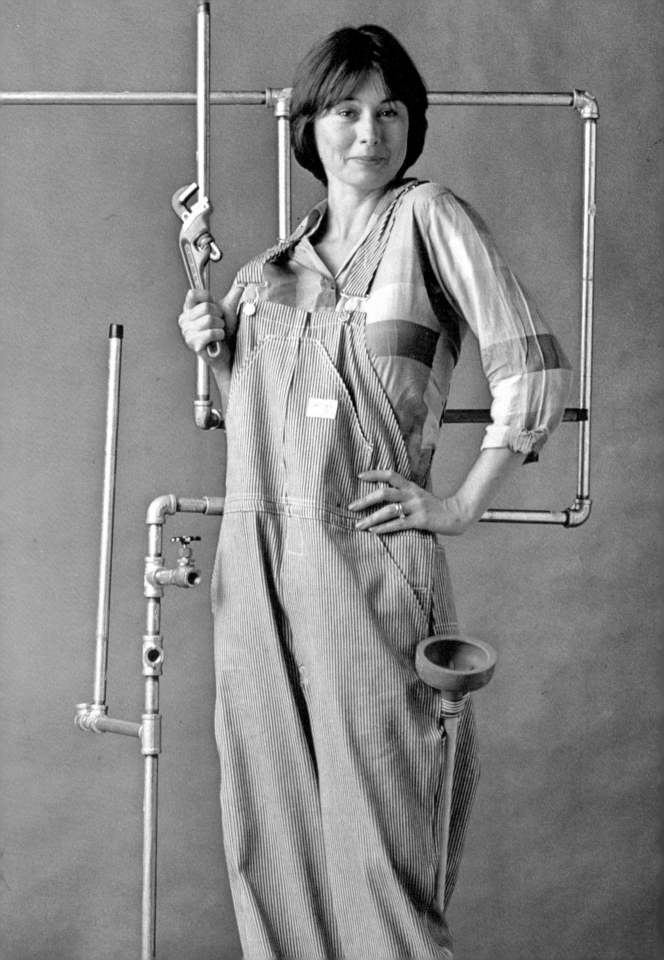

When Plumbing Goes Wrong

4

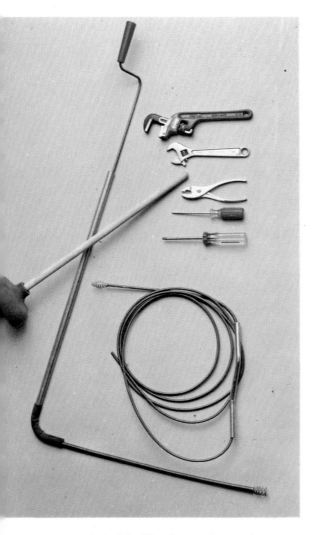

Above: the tools for Ms. Plumber are few and simple. Besides the Survival Kit, which will handle most emergencies, you may need a pipe wrench, a snake, and a closet auger. These last two help clear deep stoppages in sink drains and toilets.

Left: the triumphant home plumber. Pipes are no mystery to her—and you can conquer them, too.

Most plumbers report that nearly two-thirds of their service calls are for minor repairs that could easily have been handled by any reasonably handy amateur. To me, that means any woman who can handle a screwdriver. To you, it should mean you can save money by doing many small plumbing repairs yourself.

The first thing you should learn about doing your own plumbing is where to find the main shutoff valve that controls the water supply for your house. In most cases this valve will be located in some dark corner of the basement, or utility room, near the water meter. Once you find the valve, label it clearly so that every other member of the house can find it when necessary.

Patching Leaky Pipes

A leak in a water pipe is the signal for prompt action. Obviously, your first step is to stop the flow of water by closing the appropriate supply valve. If the leak is more than a pinpoint hole, you'll be glad you know which valve to turn. Beyond putting a pan under the leak and emptying it every half hour, the simplest of all temporary repairs can be made with ordinary plastic tape wrapped around the outside of the pipe. This will work on simple pinhole leaks, but the tape won't hold unless you dry the outside of the pipe completely, and wrap two or three overlapping spiral layers over the leaky section.

Epoxy patching compound will make permanent repairs on copper, steel, brass, and other metals. Epoxy plastic materials harden overnight to form a repair that will easily withstand normal household water pressures. Epoxy repairs and patches are permanent. If you seal a joint or union with epoxy, it cannot be unsealed later on.

Most hardware stores carry commercial pipe clamps similar to the one illustrated. They come in kits—sized for the diameter of the pipe to be fixed—consisting of a clamp and a sheet of rubber. Cover the hole with the sheet rubber (a piece of old inner tube or rubber matting will also work). Then tighten

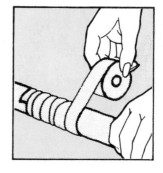 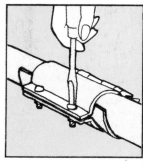

Sweating pipes occur when cold water in them condenses moisture in the air around them, much as moisture gathers on an iced drink glass. Cure the problem by wrapping insulation around the pipes. Dry the pipes thoroughly before starting to wrap.

A leaky pipe will have to be replaced sooner or later, but can be fixed temporarily with wrappings of electrical tape.

The best method for stopping pipe leaks is a commercial pipe clamp and rubber blanket. They come in packaged kits.

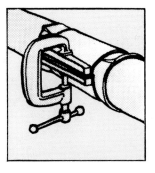 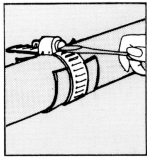 

In an emergency, improvise a clamp. This one is a C-clamp, tin from a can, and rubber from a bicycle tire tube.

Hose clamps stop leaks on pipes of any size. If your emergency is at the weekend, you can get a hose at a gas station.

Epoxy putty can be used to stop leaks in places where clamps won't fit. Pipe must be dry. Follow instructions on the can.

the clamp over it. Bear down hard when tightening the nuts. A similar repair can be made with a hose clamp. If you look at the hoses connecting your washing machine to the water supply, you will find two of the little gadgets just like the one illustrated. In an emergency, take one off, and use it with any bit of rubber sheet you can find— possibly a piece cut from a bike tire inner tube, or any other inner tube.

Fixing Leaky Faucets

All household faucets, regardless of their design or age, work on the same general principles. But while the principle is the same, I've found that the newer type, single faucets are beyond my skills. Fortunately, they don't very often leak. When they do, you can usually manage to disassemble the faucet, and buy a complete new inner unit to make the repair.

If your sinks, tubs, and showers have two faucets, however, 20 minutes of work and a five-cent washer will stop that annoying drip, drip, drip. The first thing that comes to mind when a faucet drips is to use plenty of muscle to tighten the handle. What you're actually doing is making things worse by grinding to bits against the inside of the faucet a piece of rubber called the "stem" washer. The proper thing to do is to put in a new washer.

There are two kinds of easy-to-fix faucet leaks: dripping from the spout, and leaking around the stem. If you have invested in your

Home Survival Kit, you have the necessary tools on hand—an adjustable crescent wrench, all-purpose pliers, screwdriver, and an assortment of washers. Take a few minutes to study the exploded faucet diagram on page 50, and you are ready to go to work.

Curing Drips

1. Since you will have to remove the faucet stem, there will be nothing to shut off the water while you are replacing the washer; so reach underneath the sink, and turn off the valve under the leaky faucet. Turn the faucet on to make sure you shut the right valve. If it's the faucet that drips, and the tube is recessed or set flush to the floor, the valves may be in the basement or utility room. The most likely location is near the hot water heater.

2. There are a lot of small parts to come off— particularly two very important little screws.

3. Now take the handle off. This requires removing the screw that holds it on. If you cannot find the screw at the top of the faucet handle, it is under the little "H" or "C" button. This usually snaps off if you lift it with a screwdriver. On older faucets, it may unscrew. The handle should now lift off. If it doesn't, give it a few taps—not whacks— with the handle of your screwdriver. If the handle has been in place for a number of years, it may be corroded. A few drops of penetrating oil (even sewing machine oil) may loosen it enough to tap off.

4. Next you have to remove the packing, or bonnet nut. If the faucet unit is made of bright chrome, wrap tape around the packing nut, and loosen it with either a crescent wrench or adjustable wrench. Occasionally the packing nut is covered with a decorative bell-shaped housing called a bonnet. It may be held on with a flat nut on top. Remove this nut with your wrench, and slide the bonnet off. Now loosen and remove the packing nut along with the valve stem or spindle. Once the nut is loosened, this unit removes quite easily. If it doesn't, you may have to put the handle back on and use it as a wrench, or even to unscrew the spindle.

5. At the bottom of the spindle there is a small brass screw holding the worn washer. Remove the screw, and lift the old washer from the stem with your screwdriver. The little screw may be in so tight that you can't get it out with your screwdriver, or repeated washer changes may have so worn the slot that your screwdriver won't hold. Don't despair. Use your knife and/or a beer can opener to cut and scrape the old washer out. The screw will now stick up so that you can grip it with the end of your all-purpose pliers, and unscrew it.

6. From your assortment of washers, select a new one that is the same size as the old. Put in the new washer, and screw it down tight. If the old screw was worn, replace it too. Put everything back in place in the reverse order from which you removed it. This should solve most faucet drips.

Leaks Around the Stem

1. The first thing to do is to try to tighten the packing nut with your crescent wrench. A half turn or so should do the trick.

2. If not, or if you have to set the packing nut so tight you can't turn the water on, you have to remove the nut, and replace the packing inside.

3. Repeat the steps for replacing washers to the point of removing the bonnet, or cone nut. Inside the nut you will find a rubber or plastic ring, and/or something that appears to be a greasy, gray string. This string is

called packing. You can buy rolls of it at the hardware store; in a pinch you can use ordinary twine. If the ring is worn, replace it. (Some are especially made, and you may have trouble finding one to fit. If so, remove the entire stem assembly, and take it to a plumbing supplier. He can probably give you a replacement.) If the nut was packed, repack it by winding a few turns around the top of the faucet stem, just above the threads that engage the packing nut.

4. Reassemble and test. Still leaking? Then you need a plumber.

While the repairs I've described work well for most installations of two faucets, the working parts of faucets on showers are some-

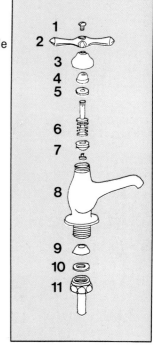

Although faucets differ widely in appearance, the insides are much the same. When you dismantle a faucet in your home, you will recognize parts similar to these shown.

1 Handle screw
2 Handle
3 Cap, or bonnet, nut
4 Packing
5 Bib washer
6 Spindle
7 Stem, or seat, washer and screw
8 Faucet body
9-11 Connections to water supply

times recessed so that you can't get at them with an ordinary wrench. Should you have a dripping shower head, you may need a tool called a *socket wrench* to reach the packing nut. It will cost a few dollars—perhaps $3 or more—but it's still cheaper than having the plumber come.

Toilet Troubles

Here is one sure place you should apply Fixit Rule 2 of studying your problem before

To dismantle a faucet, first shut off water below sink. Remove cap over handle screw, if any.

Remove handle. Many handle screws require that you use a Phillips screwdriver on them.

Next step is to remove cap nut. If you wrap it with tape, you will prevent it from scratching.

Now lift out spindle. If it doesn't come out easily, replace handle and use it as your wrench.

Faucet washer is at end of spindle. Remove the screw, put it carefully aside, lift out washer.

If the screw is corroded, you may have to cut the washer out first, and then remove screw.

Select replacement washer of same size from Survival Kit assortment.

Put replacement washer in place on spindle, and screw it down tight. If screw is worn, replace it, too.

Reassemble the faucet parts in exactly the reverse order of disassembling. Turn faucet to off position, and open the faucet below sink.

doing anything. If you take the lid off the tank and watch what happens when you flush, the whole complicated contraption becomes simple and logical. All those levers and floats actually make up two valves. One, called the flush valve, consists of a rubber ball (the tank ball) or flapper that holds water in the tank until it is lifted by the action of twisting the handle. The other, called the inlet, or *ballcock* valve, is connected to the water supply to fill the tank again. The ball that floats on the water is attached to the arm that controls the ballcock, opening it when it's down, closing it when it rises.

Here's how it works:

1. When you flip the handle, a lever lifts

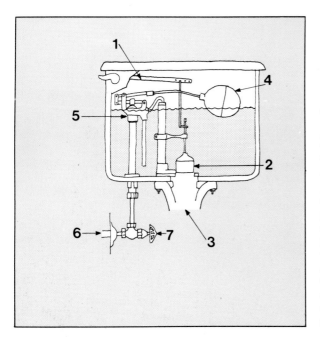

the tank ball, opening the outlet so the water rushes from the tank into the toilet bowl.

2. As the tank empties, the tank ball slowly falls back into place, closing the opening so the tank can fill again.

3. The float ball drops with the water. This opens the ballcock, and fresh water enters. Most of it goes into the tank but some goes into the toilet bowl through a little hose or copper pipe running into the overflow pipe.

4. As the water level rises, so does the float ball, gradually closing the ballcock valve until it shuts off entirely when the tank is full.

Most of the common annoying problems with toilets involve either one or the other of the two valves. They are easy to repair.

The Ever-Running Toilet

If after flushing the tank does not refill, yet water continues running into the bowl, the trouble is in the rubber tank ball or its seat. In most cases the tank ball will be worn so that it does not fit properly against its seat. You will have to replace the ball.

1. Shut off the water supply to the toilet tank. If the shutoff valve is so worn you can't turn it off, tie the float ball arm as high as it will go with a piece of string tied to a stick placed across the tank. This will shut off the water.

2. Now flush the tank; then reach in and unscrew the ball from its wire guide. Before you replace it with a new one, clean the valve seat by scrubbing it lightly with fine steel wool. If the wire guide is corroded or bent, it may be a good idea to give it a scrubbing, too, or install a new one.

3. Turn the water back on, and check the flushing operation. If the new ball does not seat properly, it may not be centered. This can be caused by a bent wire guide. If so, replace it. If the guide arm is out of alignment, you can adjust it easily. Loosen the set screw that holds it in place, and then jiggle the guide arm back and forth until the ball drops directly into place.

The Whistler

When the tank fills properly after flushing, but water continues to pour in until it goes out through the overflow pipe with a whistling noise, the trouble is in either the float ball mechanism, or in the ballcock valve itself.

1. Try lifting the float ball arm slightly with one finger. If this stops the whistling noise, and shuts off the water flow, the float ball is either leaking and needs replacing, or its arm needs adjusting.

2. Unscrew the float ball, and give it a shake to see whether there is any water inside. If

Above: before attempting to fix a toilet tank, apply fixit Rule 1. Open the tank, examine the parts, and observe what happens during the flush and refill.

there is, the ball must be replaced. Buy a plastic one, because it will last a lifetime. If the ball isn't leaky, the float arm needs adjustment.

3. Try bending the wire arm slightly downward in the middle so that the ball is about a half-inch lower inside the tank. Then turn the water on, and try flushing again. This time the water should shut off when it rises to within one inch below the top of the overflow pipe. If it still continues to rise, try bending the float arm a little lower.

4. If all this fails to shut off the flow of water, adjusting the float arm or replacing the ball will be of no avail. The trouble is then in the ballcock itself. This is a plumber's job.

The Too Dainty Flush

If too little water flows into the bowl to clean it out satisfactorily, you may be faced with one of three problems.

1. Most likely the tank ball is seating too soon because its guide is set too low. Loosen the screws that secure the guide arm to the overflow tube, and raise it about a half-inch. This allows the tank ball to float longer before it drops into its seat again.

2. Once in a while an inadequate flush can be caused by the float ball being adjusted too low to let the tank fill all the way. Bend the

Ballcock operation can be regulated by bending float ball arm up or down. This can be done easily without removing ballcock from tank.

Left: boiling water— lots of it—can sometimes dissolve grease to open a sluggish drain.

Right: caustic cleansers for drains must not be used until sink has already drained. Routine monthly applications of drain cleanser will help prevent a build-up of grease in the sink trap.

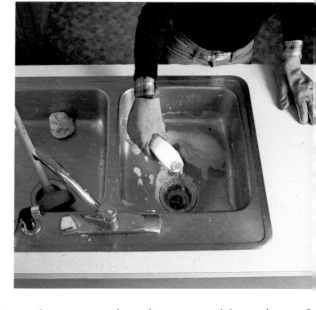

float arm upward. This is the reverse of treating the whistler.

3. An inadequate flush may also be caused by clogged outlet ports around the underside of the rim. This is a fairly common trouble in hard water areas. While this condition is not easy to cure, it can help to scrub the ports vigorously with a stiff brush. If this doesn't work, try reaming the ports with a piece of stiff, fine wire. If the bowl empties sluggishly, the trouble is in the drain rather than the tank, and can be remedied.

Clearing Clogged Drains

When your sinks or tub start to drain slowly, it's a sure sign that an obstruction is building

Before using plumber's helper to open clogged sink, be sure to remove the stopper from outlet.

Another step before use of plumber's helper is to stuff overflow opening with wet washcloth.

If sink drain cannot be opened by plunging action of plumber's helper, you will have to dismantle the trap. It's a good idea to turn off the inlet valve just in case you have to leave the job before it's completed.

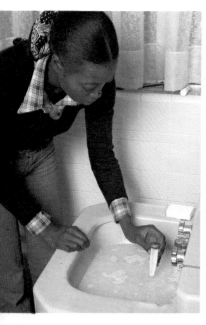

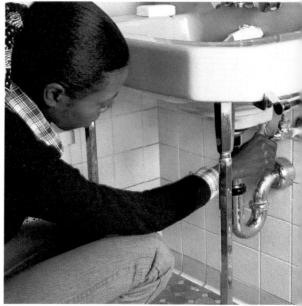

up somewhere along the drain pipes, and you're soon going to be in for a stopped-up drain.

Getting at the problem right away with a can of chemical drain cleaner, or a kettle of boiling water, may save you the work and trouble of removing the waste trap pipe under the sink. (If you have a septic tank disposal system, be sure to use the type of chemical drain cleaner that will not stop the bacterial action in the septic tank. Check the label on the can.)

Caution: if the drain is completely blocked, don't attempt to ladle out some of the water to pour a chemical cleaner into the drain pipe. In most cases the cleaner won't reach the obstruction, and may form a hard deposit that leaves you with an even worse stoppage.

Clogged Sinks

1. Clean the strainer or lint trap in the drain to clear it of hair, chunks of soap, or bits of food.

2. If this doesn't work, try reaching through the water, and placing the palm of your hand over the open drain. Pump up and down with your palm, making a slight force. This may push the obstruction through, and start the water draining. Should these two quick remedies fail, you will have to turn to the "plumber's helper," or force cup (see Chapter 2).

3. Jam a rag into the overflow opening in the bowl of the sink, and remove the lint trap or sink strainer if there is one. Place the plumber's helper over the open drain. Hold the wooden handle in both hands, and press it down suddenly to create a force. Repeat about a dozen times. This may break up the clog. If you can get the sink to drain completely, even if slowly, then try an application of drain cleaner to finish the job.

4. If Step 3 fails, try to clean out the elbow trap beneath the sink. Place an empty pail or pan under the trap. If the trap has a plug, unscrew it. If there is no plug, remove the whole trap by loosening the two fittings on either side of the curving elbow. This will call for a pipe wrench. Be careful because water and globs of hair and other matter may come out with a whoosh when the plug or trap is removed. If the trap is clogged up,

Place a pan under the sink just in case water comes pouring out when the trap is removed.

If stoppage isn't in the trap, your next step is to use a plumber's snake. Force it into the drain.

The plumber's snake is designed so that you can feed it in by pushing and twisting. This is not an easy job and several tries may be needed just to get the snake going down into the drain.

ream it out with a wire—a straightened out coat hanger does nicely. But if the trap is clear, your problem lies between the elbow and the sink itself. Poke and probe around through the pipe between sink and elbow with your piece of wire. If this gets results, give the pipe and trap a good scrubbing with a bottle brush and lots of hot water.

5. Reassemble the trap, making sure it is tight, and test. If the reassembled trap leaks at either fitting, try tightening them. Should it still leak, take it apart again, and make sure the packing washers are in place. That should solve your problem.

6. If the stoppage is not in the trap nor between trap and sink, it may lie between the trap and the place where the pipe disappears into the wall. Try probing and pushing with your straightened coat hanger. There is just a slight chance this may work. If not, you can either give up and call the plumber now, or have one more go with the tool called a plumber's snake. Feed it in slowly, twisting and cranking. You should try to get several feet of it into the drain. I warn you that it is not easy, but it can be done. If you meet with success, the snake will stop, and then suddenly push through. When you pull it out, you will find its spiral end covered with a messy substance of some kind.

7. If all fails, admit defeat, and make a call to a plumber.

The Clogged Toilet Bowl

This most unfortunate of all household emergencies almost invariably happens without prior warning. But, if you should happen to notice the toilet is draining slowly, apply emergency methods before the thing clogs up entirely.

1. Since a toilet bowl stoppage usually results in an overflow, the first step, after shutting off the inlet valve, is mopping up. Don't try to remedy the situation with another flush or two.

2. If the clogging substance—most often a large wad of toilet paper—is visible, the simple and direct remedy is to reach in and pull it out. For the sake of hygiene you can

Above: if you apply the plumber's helper with vigor—and many times—you will usually be able to unclog toilet drain.

Right: you've done it yourself, and saved the time, trouble, and money of a call to a plumber.

put a plastic bag over your hand and arm. Even if the source of the clogging is not visible, try reaching down toward the trap to see if you can locate the stuff, and pull it out by hand.

3. If these first-aid methods do not produce results, the chances are good that your trusty plumber's helper will. Bail out some of the water so as to prevent an overflow, and work away, making sure that the cup is located directly over the outlet. Push hard, using both hands, and all the muscle you've got. Don't give up too soon. If your first

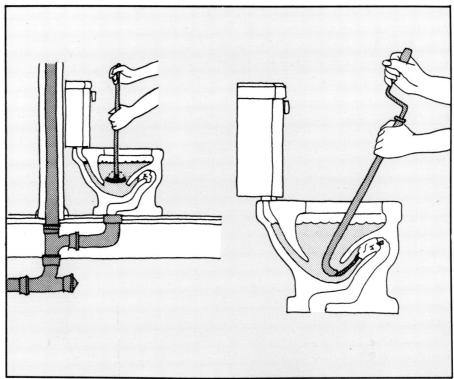

Above: diagram shows two ways of clearing a clogged toilet bowl. The easier way is with a plumber's helper, but if that doesn't work, a closet auger might do.

Right: a closet auger may have to be fed into the toilet trap by hand, which is not much fun. It also takes patience and perseverance, but may get results that save you a service call.

dozen plunges don't produce results, try another 12—and yet another.

4. Still no results? Now you have a choice. Call the plumber, or try the variant of the snake called a "closet auger." This tool will reach down into the trap, and grind what's stuck in there to bits, or entangle it and pull it out. A closet auger, which you probably won't have until you need it, costs about $3. It's cheaper than a plumber, and usually works. The unpleasant part of it is that you will have to reach into the bowl to guide the end to the trap.

Electrical Repairs Made Easy

5

Even if you are fully convinced that you will never be able to do electrical repairs, you must know where the main service entry is located, and how to change a fuse or reset a tripped circuit breaker.

Any woman who can change a light bulb—and that surely includes most of us—can do small electrical repairs around her home. When a fuse blows, you can trace the cause, and correct it. Balky, nonringing doorbells can be fixed easily. Broken light switches can be replaced without trouble. You can even replace an outlet.

Before you try any electrical repairs,

however, there are some rules you should learn and follow. Otherwise your experience may be a shocking one.

1. Never attempt to repair any appliance before you unplug it from the outlet. No exceptions whatever.

2. Do not touch or turn on electrical appliances when your hands or feet are wet. Never.

3. Do not attempt to repair any switches or outlets, or change a fuse, when any part of your body is in contact with water, damp floors, or a plumbing fixture.

4. Before changing a fuse or repairing a switch or outlet, always be sure that you shut off the power.

Electricity enters your home through a "service entry." This is a box containing the main switches, and the fuses or switches called circuit breakers. Circuit breakers protect the individual circuits, and shut off the power when they are carrying an overload of electrical current. When you plug in too many appliances on one circuit, or if one of the appliances has defective wiring, the fuse will blow, or the circuit breaker will shut itself off.

Every member of the household, including older children, should know where the service entry is, and how to shut off the main power supply. Apartment dwellers should ask the superintendent where their fuse box is. You should also know which circuit in your home or apartment is controlled by each fuse or circuit breaker. It is a good idea to label each circuit.

Shorts and Overloads

Each circuit has been planned to carry a certain number of lights and appliances. When you go beyond that limit by plugging in more, the demand for power overloads the circuit. That's when the fuse will blow, or the circuit breaker will trip, or switch off. Should two bare wires touch somewhere in the circuit or in an appliance, a situation known as a "short" or "short circuit" develops. When this happens, electricity flows through the circuit without being used

59

by appliances. This results in a rapid over-load that will also blow fuses, and trip the circuit breakers.

Replacing Fuses

When a part of your house suddenly loses power—usually immediately after you have turned something on, or plugged in an appliance—a fuse has blown, and it requires replacement. Before you start, however, unplug all the appliances in that circuit, and turn off all switches.

Never—even in an emergency—replace a blown fuse with one of higher rating. With the right fuse in hand, proceed as follows :

1. Look in the fuse box for the blown fuse. Its glass window will show a black, burnt-looking smudge.
2. Select a new fuse that matches.
3. Turn off the main power. Unscrew the blown fuse, and replace it.
4. Turn the main power on.

Caution : if your fuse box is located in the basement—and your basement floor is damp, even a little—you should stand on a rubber bathmat before opening the box, or touching the main switch.

Should the new fuse blow immediately, the problem is in the main wiring. Don't attempt another replacement, but call the

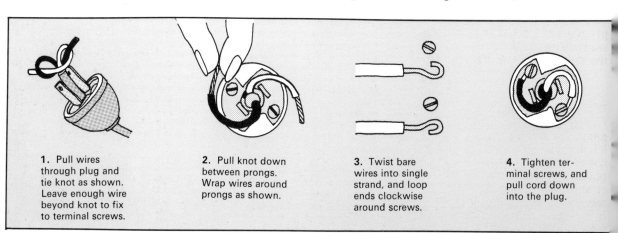

1. Pull wires through plug and tie knot as shown. Leave enough wire beyond knot to fix to terminal screws.

2. Pull knot down between prongs. Wrap wires around prongs as shown.

3. Twist bare wires into single strand, and loop ends clockwise around screws.

4. Tighten terminal screws, and pull cord down into the plug.

Left: you can tell these fuses are good because the metal strips beneath the windows are intact. The strip will be broken and the window smudged in a burned-out fuse.

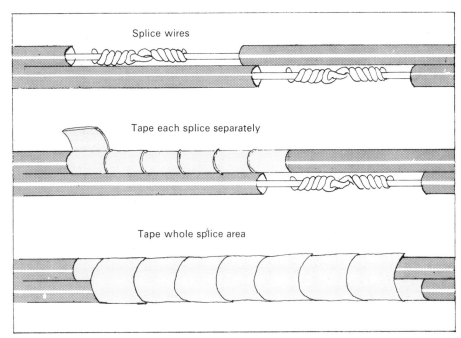

Splice wires

Tape each splice separately

Tape whole splice area

Right: diagram shows a spliced wire. In the top drawing, wires have been twisted together. Next, one wire has been well wrapped with insulating tape. Last, both wires, each wrapped individually, are joined with two more layers of tape.

electricity company or serviceman. Right away. Chances are, however, that the fuse won't blow a second time. So, if you remember which appliance or light you turned on when the fuse went, (and you should) turn on all but the offender, one by one. Everything should be fine.

If occurrences of this kind are a common event around your place, it's a sure sign that the wiring and circuit planning is not up to the demands you are putting on them. For safety's sake as well as for convenience, your house should be rewired.

Now that you know how to switch the main power off and on again, and which

fuses or circuit breakers control the principal circuits and major appliances, you have all the basic electrical knowledge you need.

Rewiring a Plug
When an appliance or lamp won't work, and you're sure you have it plugged in and turned on, then the problem may be either in the outlet, or the plug itself.

1. Check the outlet either with your circuit tester, or by plugging in another lamp or appliance. No results? Then the outlet needs repairing. (See page 68.) If the test shows that the outlet is delivering power, try step 2 to get better contact.

Left: it is easy to replace the plug on extension cords if you follow the steps in the diagram.

Right: shown here are two types of replacement plugs. The one on the left is a clip-on plug; it is extremely easy to put on, but is not as strong as the standard replacement plug, shown on the right, and explained in the diagram.

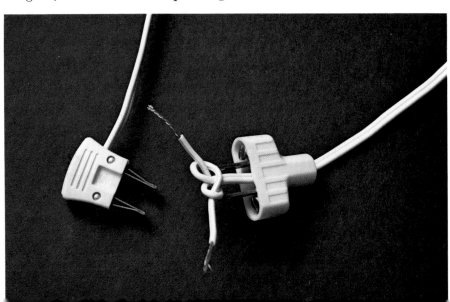

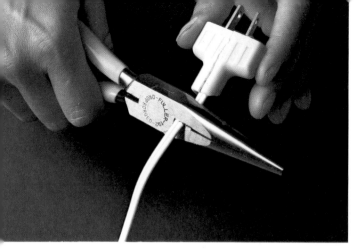

Above: the first step in replacing a standard plug with the clip-on variety begins with cutting off the defective plug. Make a good, clean cut.

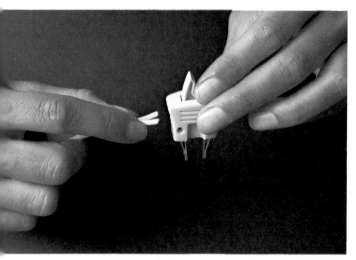

Above: separate the wires for ¾ of an inch. Do not bare ends. Open clamp of replacement plug and insert wires into plug holes just as shown. Below: push the wires in as far as they will go. Hold plug firmly, and press the clamp down tightly until it snaps into place. Done in minutes!

2. Gently bend the two prongs of the plug slightly apart. This should give a better contact, and may be all that is needed. If not, the problem is inside the plug.

3. Look at the plug. If the prongs stick up through a fiber disk, lift it off with a screwdriver. Make sure that one of the wires under the small screws has not worked loose. If this has happened, wrap the wire clockwise under the screw, and tighten.

4. If the prongs are sealed in a rubber or plastic body so that you can't get at them, and the prongs are loose or the plug is cracked, you will have to buy a new cord, or replace the plug. Since the business end of the cords on many lamps disappear inside, replacement is usually the necessary step.

1. With your electrician's pliers cut off the plug and at least an inch of cord, removing all the broken or cracked portion of the cord.

2. Strip off two inches of insulation from the end of the cord. Do this carefully so that when the two individual wires are exposed, their insulation is not damaged. Use a jacknife or single-edge razor blade. If the cord has two wires with rubber molded over them, split the two sections apart for about two inches.

3. Strip off about ½ to ¾ inch of insulation from each wire, which will expose many little wires. Twist these into two single strand wires.

4. Push both wires through the small end of the new plug. Tie a knot above the exposed wires, as shown in the photo on page 61.

5. Pull this knot back into the plug, nesting it in between the two prongs.

6. Hook one of the stranded wires around each prong, and wrap wires clockwise around the closest terminal screw. Tighten the screws.

When you are dealing with lamp cords and some light appliance cords, however, there is a much easier way. Simply buy a plug that can, in one way or another, be clipped onto the cut ends of the cord. This easy method of plug repair eliminates both the stripping of the wires, and making them fast to the terminal screws.

Caution: after you have repaired a cord this way, never pull the plug by means of the wire.

The Appliance Plug

Today, more and more appliances come with their cords fastened directly to the appliance itself. Some, however, have at the appliance end of the cord a plug that slips over prongs in a socket on the appliance itself. These plugs have to take a lot of hard wear, and, because they are often made of brittle materials, are subject to cracking and chipping.

If you have a cord that is in questionable condition, my advice is to throw it away, and buy a new one. The only problem is that replacement cords don't always fit. If this happens, you may have no choice but to make the repair, for which the easy directions follow.

Repairing a Damaged Cord

Cords are subject to wear. Sooner or later the fabric becomes worn and frayed, or the rubber becomes brittle and cracked. Either situation is potentially dangerous, calling either for a new cord, or a repair. When the cord is integral to an appliance that you don't want to take out of service for too long, repair is in order. Here's how you go about it:

1. If fabric-covered cord is frayed, but the wires beneath do not show through, wrap the cord with two layers of insulating tape. Start an inch or so on one side of the frayed area, and carry the wrap an inch or so beyond.

2. If rubber-coated or fabric cords are frayed to the point where the inner wires show, use your electrician's pliers to cut out the worn spot. Cut one wire shorter or longer than the other so that their repairs won't be directly opposite. (Before you do this with fabric-covered ends, strip off the upper layer of insulation.) This method produces a stronger repair, and is less bulky.

3. With the pliers, a jackknife, or single-edge razor blade, strip off two inches of

Above: replacement of broken plug at appliance end of cord—whether it has a switch or not—is similar to the technique of replacing wall plug.

Above: with replacement plug on hand, open defective plug by removing screws. Then unscrew the terminal screws, and lift out the wires.

Below: open replacement plug, and loosen its terminal screws. Loop the wires clockwise around screws, and tighten. Reassemble the plug case.

There's a lot of work in fixing a broken lamp socket, but it's not really hard, and the money you can save with this kind of repair is well worth the effort.

Left: first disconnect the lamp from its socket, then take the lamp apart by removing the nut in the base. This nut holds the metal tube inside.

insulation from each of the four cut ends. Twist the exposed fine wires into four single strands.

4. Join the two strands from each side of the original cut by twisting them together, and wrap each wire with insulating tape ; carry the tape beyond the union. When you are finished there should not be the slightest sign of bare wire.

5. Wrap all the wires together with two more layers of tape.

Repairing a Lamp Switch

When a lamp begins to give you trouble, there are three possible causes.

1. The outlet plug has gone bad. Test by plugging the lamp in another outlet. If it works perfectly, you may want to change the bad outlet. (See page 68).

2. The switch or socket has gone bad. This is usually indicated by trouble in getting the lamp to stay on, or when the switch has to be snapped two or three times. Fluttering, of course, could be caused by a loose bulb. You have checked that, haven't you ?

3. The cord is worn or broken nearly through inside the lamp, or it has come loose from one of the terminal screws on the switch socket.

Pull tube up. Unscrew socket from top of tube. Remove outer shell and insulating sleeve from socket. Unscrew wires at terminals. Remove the defective socket.

Disassemble replacement socket. Pull the wire through cap, and tie a knot (see page 60). Twist strands to make single wires, and loop each wire clockwise around terminal screws.

Make sure that terminal screws are tight, and strands from opposite wires do not touch each other or metal of socket.

Replace the insulating sleeve of the socket.

Replace outer shell and snap onto cap. Put bulb into socket, and test. If bulb lights, lamp is ready for reassembly. If not, the trouble may be in cord. Use these photos as your guide for replacing a bad cord.

Replacing the Switch and Socket

1. Buy a replacement socket. They are all standard, and any one will fit your lamp.

2. Assemble your tools: pliers, both all-purpose and electrical, and screwdriver. Unplug the lamp and apply Rule 2 to get the old socket loose. This may take some doing. Because you have to be able to pull up through the lamp several inches of the cord to work with, you may have to disassemble the base. That's why you need Rule 2, and the all-purpose pliers.

3. When you have the old socket loose from the lamp base, and pulled up so you can work with it, examine it carefully. There are usually several parts that make the union between lamp base and the socket. The wire must go through all of them.

4. On the socket you will find the word "press". Do so—hard—and it will separate. Pull out the inside, and examine the wires at the terminal screws. If they are loose, tighten them. Reassemble the socket, put in a bulb, and test. If all is okay, put the lamp back together.

5. If not, remove the old socket and replace, following the procedure for handling the wires I outlined in the plug replacement section. Reassemble the socket. Don't forget the cardboard liner. Reassemble the lamp.

Replacing a Lamp Cord

Good lamps last a long time, but over the years, the rubber insulation of the cord may become brittle and crack because of the heat of the lamp. So when you have the lamp disassembled to replace the socket, examine the cord. If it shows any signs of wear close to the socket, I suggest replacing it completely.

The trick is getting the cord through the tube that runs up inside the lamp base. I have threaded it through, but this is about as troublesome as mending socks with cooked spaghetti. The solution is simple. Take the socket apart as described above. Remove the wires from the terminal screws. Now get a piece of stout string several inches longer than the lamp base. Tie the string to a wire with

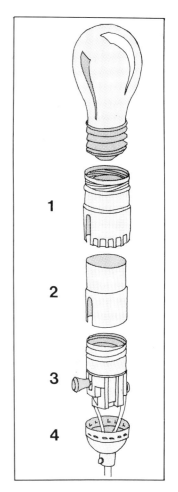

Above: lamp socket parts
1 Outer socket shell
2 Insulating sleeve
3 Socket
4 Socket cap

The broken lamp, reassembled and in good working order, is now as good as new—and the repair parts cost all of 60 cents. You could not have bought nearly as nice a lamp for less than $5.

a strong knot, and pull the wire out through the base. Tie the new cord on, and pull it back through. Now complete the job as described in replacing the socket, and re-assemble the lamp.

Putting a Switch on a Long Cord

I have some large table lamps whose switches are a nuisance to reach inside their long shades. I solved the problem by putting a switch on the wire. If you would like to follow suit, buy one of the clamp-on switches similar to that shown in the photograph on page 61, and proceed as follows:

1. Turn the lamp on with the regular socket switch. Then unplug it.

2. At some convenient place along the cord where you want the switch to be, split the cord into two separate wires. Cut carefully through the mid-line with a single-edge blade. Take care not to expose any base wire.

3. With your pliers cut *one* of the wires through. Do not strip.

4. Take the switch apart by removing the small screw. Lay the solid wire in the channel that runs from one end to the other. Lay in the cut ends so that they butt up against the dividing wall.

5. Press the upper half of the switch on firmly. Screw the parts together. Now you can turn the lamp on or off by rotating the wheel on the mid-line switch.

Replacing a Wall Switch

Now we are going to move to the next stage of electrical repairs, and replace a wall switch.

This may seem scary because we have to deal with the basic wiring of the house or apartment. However, the mechanical part of the job is no more complicated than replacing a plug or large socket. In effect, you turn off the power to the switch by pulling the appropriate fuse or circuit breaker. Even if you've labeled the circuits as suggested on page 59, test the switch to make sure that whatever it controls goes out or off. It's always best to do these repairs in daylight, but if the room is not well lighted by the sun, you'll need a flashlight.

1. Remove the outside plate by undoing the screw or screws. Now you'll see the switch.

2. Take out the top and bottom screws to free the switch so that you can pull it out to get to the wires. Here, possibly for the first time, you'll meet wires of different colors, one black, one white or red. Usually only two are connected to the switch. These wires are the mainstay of all home wiring. The black wire is "hot". If you run into extra wires (usually red), this is because your switch does more than simply turn one thing on and off. For instance, whatever you turn on in one place you can turn off at some other place, with another switch. Take careful note of how the wires are connected to the switch, and put them back the same way on the new switch.

If you have any doubts about the replacement switch you need, take the old switch to the hardware or electrical supply store, with a note of where the wires connect to it, and what color they are. Your new switch can be a plain replacement, or you can change to a noiseless mercury, or a dimmer switch. Dimmers, however, are for lights only. Do not try to use them where the switch also controls an outlet that might be used for appliances.

3. Before you attempt to remove the wires from the old switch, or even touch any metal part, use your circuit tester to make sure the power is really off. Place the terminals of the tester on the terminal screws of the switch. If the tester glows, stop. Either you have not turned off the power in the circuit, or, because of cross wiring, power is still leaking through. Turn off the main power. Now proceed to loosen the terminal screws, and remove the switch.

4. Hook the black wire(s) to the dark brassy looking side of the new switch, and the white wire(s) to the light silvery side of it. Tighten

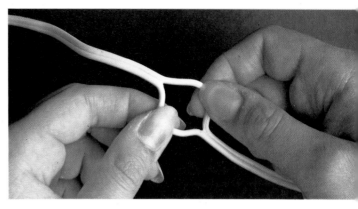

The first step in installing a mid-wire switch is to separate the wires (above). The second step is to cut through only one of the wires (below).

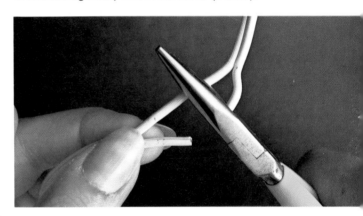

Open the mid-wire switch by removing the central screw, and then lay the wires in (below). Reassemble the two halves of the switch (bottom). The pressure of the screw will drive contacts in wire.

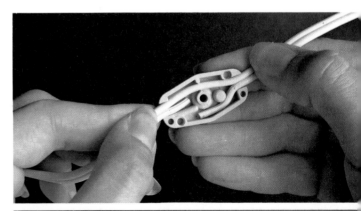

Right: before you do anything to replace a defective wall switch, defuse the circuit, or trip the circuit breaker to off position. Remove the switch face plate.

Next, test switch with circuit tester. If it lights, there is power in the circuit, and you should not proceed. Check fuses again to defuse the right one.

and fold the extra wire behind the switch. Press switch, wires and all, back into the metal box. Replace the top and bottom screws, then the cover plate. Turn power on.

Now remove screws at top and bottom of the switch, and pull it out of the wall receptacle.

Replacing Wall Outlets

The problem with small appliances and lamps that don't work may be in the outlet rather than in the appliance plug, cord, or switch. Inside the slots of the outlet are two metal terminals. Sometimes—although rarely—they become loose or worn so that they do not make a solid contact with the plug.

If testing your lamp or other appliances indicates that the outlet is at fault, you can change it yourself. Before doing so, however, test it again by inserting the metal ends of your circuit tester in the slots as far as you can push them. If the bulb glows steadily, then

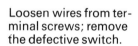

Loosen wires from terminal screws; remove the defective switch.

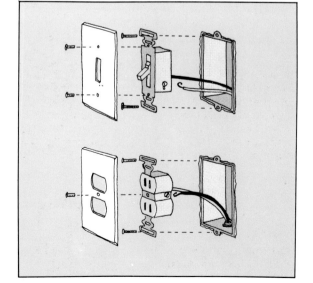

Above: schematic for switch and outlet replacement.

Use pliers to bend wires around terminal screws of new switch, and fasten them in tightly.

You will not pull the switch out like this. It is done in this photo only to demonstrate re-wiring technique. Compare with the diagram.

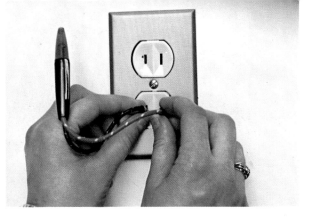

Left: before you replace wall outlet, be sure it is defective by checking it with a circuit tester.

Right: turn off power in circuit. Remove face plate. Check with circuit tester to make sure electrical power is off.

Remove screws, and lift outlet out of receptacle.

the outlet is okay. The problem lies somewhere in the appliance. If the tester does not glow, you need a new outlet. An electrician will charge you $10 to make the change. You can do it yourself for the cost of a new outlet, which is less than a dollar.

To replace a faulty outlet, you will go about it much as you did for the wall switch.

1. Turn off the power, remove the outside plate, and undo the screws that hold the outlet in the metal receptacle.

2. Pull out the plug, and retest with the circuit tester to make sure the power is off. You're likely to run into extra wires. If this is the case, you'll find two whites and two blacks, or sometimes a red if the wall outlet is controlled by a wall switch. Study them carefully before disconnecting so you can follow the same scheme when rewiring the replacement plug. Connect them as they were on the old outlet.

Loosen wires at terminal screws, remove defective outlet, and replace it.

If your house or apartment is new the outlet will have, in addition to the two familiar slots, a large semicircular opening somewhere in the middle. Inside this opening there is a metal terminal connecting to a *ground wire*, a feature that adds safety by grounding any appliance plugged into it.

It's likely that your home is new enough that you won't have any trouble with outlet plugs for years, if ever. Should you need to replace one, however, you'll find that when you pull the outlet out of the wall it will have either *a green wire, or bare copper wire attached to a green screw*. This is the ground wire.

Some switches and outlets are designed so that wires do not hook around terminal screws, but are pushed into holes. Contact is made by tightening screws.

Follow the instructions given above for changing a two-wire outlet. Be sure, however, that you buy a "three-wire" replacement, and reconnect the ground wire.

When either switch or outlet has been removed, interior of receptacle will look like this. Notice hot black wire, and white ground wire.

Above: photos show both sides of a three-wire outlet. The procedure for replacing such outlets and switches is similar to that for two-wire fixtures. The ground wire—either bare or covered with green insulation—must be attached to green screw.

Left: beware of danger! Whoever installed this grounding adaptor in the bottom outlet has overlooked an important step. The hook must be attached behind the center screw. You will only use a grounding adaptor if the wall outlets in your house are not already grounded. If they are, they will have three holes, as in the top outlet. Ungrounded ones have two holes, into which the three-hole adaptor must be fitted.

Installing a Grounding Plug

If you're deep into the fixit business, you may have purchased an electric drill or sander, and you probably found that the plug of your new power tool has three prongs. These consist of two ordinary looking ones, and a rounded one that fits in the hole in the three-wire outlet I've just told you about. But your house isn't wired that way, and none of your outlets accept the prongs of this tool. In this case you can buy a three-wire adapter.

However, before you give it your full confidence, test it with your circuit tester. Put one terminal of the tester in one slot, and touch the center screw of the outlet face plate with the other. If the tester bulb doesn't glow, the device isn't grounded. Don't use it until you've had an electrician in to wire your outlets so they will ground.

Repairing Doorbells

When your doorbell won't ring, or won't quit ringing, there are four possible problem spots: the pushbutton, the chimes or bell, the transformer, or the wires either between the pushbutton and bell or between the transformer and bell.

The most important thing to know before you attempt any repairs on a bothersome doorbell is that the transformer (usually located on the back of the service entry box, or close to it) is there because the bell system works on low voltage—either 12 or 24 volts. The transformer cuts the standard 115-120 volt house current to this level. This makes the system safer to work on.

One side of the transformer will be connected to the service entry by heavy wires. *Never touch them.* The other side, from which small rubber- or fabric-coated wires run, delivers power to the bell and the button.

One side of the transformer will be connected to the service entry by heavy wires. *Never touch them.* The other side, from which small rubber- or fabric-coated wires run, delivers power to the bell and the button.

Near the screw terminals on the bell side, you will find a legend telling how much voltage it delivers. If it's more than 12 volts, it can give you a fairly good shaking—not dangerous, but certainly painful. I suggest that after locating the problem, you defuse the circuit before you begin working on it.

When the Bell Won't Ring

1. Check the pushbutton. It's the most common source of trouble, because its exposed location allows the contacts and wires to corrode. Unscrew the little collar or plate around the button itself, and remove it. This will expose the wires. Unscrew them from the terminals, and touch the bare tips together. If the bell rings, your problems are solved. Scrape or lightly sandpaper the wires and contacts, and reconnect the wires. If the bell still does not ring, the button will have to be replaced. Buy a new one and do it yourself. The procedure is just the same as for installing a wall switch. If the bell did not sound when the wires were touched, the trouble is elsewhere.

2. Check the bells. Make sure that each wire is securely attached to its terminals. The bell may not be getting power. Test it with a circuit tester, or by laying a piece of scrap wire across two terminals. If you get a little spark or light when you do this, there is power at the bell. The trouble may be that one of the moving parts is stuck by dirt or grease. Clean the parts. This should clear up the problem. If there is no power at the bell, turn your attention to the transformer.

3. Check the fuse or circuit breaker on the bell circuit. Replace a burned-out fuse, or reset the circuit breaker to "on". *Now, if you are absolutely sure that you are working on the low voltage side*, lay the bare tip of your screwdriver across the terminals. If the transformer is working properly, a small spark will jump. Even better, use your circuit tester. If the transformer isn't working, call an electrician.

4. If there is power at the transformer, but not at the bell, there is a break in a wire somewhere between. This may be hard to find, but do what you can by following the exposed wires as far as you can. Look especially for taped areas, or places where one wire joins another. Chances are very good

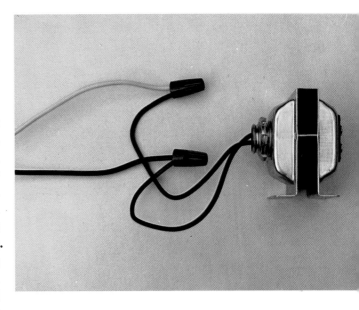

Above: a transformer converts 120-volt alternating current to low voltage direct current for doorbells. The transformer will be located near the service entry. Work only on the side carrying low voltage—the side away from the service entry.

that the break will be where the wire has been spliced or worked. Should you find a break in the wires, or a place where the insulation has worn off, make the repair just as you would in splicing an extension cord. Be sure the wires are twisted together tightly. If you cannot locate the break, the entire length of wire will have to be replaced. This is a job for an electrician.

When the Bell Won't Quit Ringing

1. If the bell keeps on ringing, the trouble is in the pushbutton, or the wires leading from it to the bell. Probably the bell has gotten stuck. Give it a push or two to free it. Then take off the plate or collar, and brush out the inside. It may be full of dirt and dust. Put a drop of graphite around the pushbutton.

2. When inspection of the pushbutton indicates it is okay, the problem is in the wiring. Trace as much of it as you can, looking for the same problem situation suggested in tracing the wire between transformer or bell. If you can't locate the break, you need professional help.

When Major Appliances Act Up

Above left to right: when any appliance doesn't work, check first to see that it is plugged in before you call for service. If it's the washer, check to see if the water supply is on. If an appliance with a motor—such as a washer, dryer, or refrigerator—shimmies and shakes, check to see if they are level; if they aren't, level them by adjusting leveling bolts at bottom of appliance.

Below left to right: if you feel that you can get an appliance, such as a dishwasher, working better by cleaning it, refer to your owner's manual before you begin. Then follow Fixit Rules, keeping parts in order as you take them off, and remembering that parts should come off and go back into the exact same place without having to use force.

If one of your major appliances is showing peculiar symptoms, or won't work at all, chances are that you are in for a large repair bill. Before you turn your eyes heavenward and heave a sigh of resignation, there are some checks you can make. For example, has the plug been pulled out of the outlet? Has the fuse to the appliance blown, or its circuit breaker tripped because of a temporary overload? Make sure of these simple things, because appliance repairmen get rich by doing nothing more than sticking plugs back in sockets, and replacing blown fuses at almost $10 a crack.

Then, immediately check the manual.

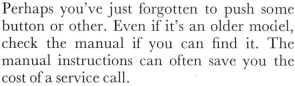

Perhaps you've just forgotten to push some button or other. Even if it's an older model, check the manual if you can find it. The manual instructions can often save you the cost of a service call.

There are times when you had better not try any fixit measures, but call for help without further ado.

Smoke: if an appliance gives off a burning odor, or begins to smoke, switch it off immediately, and disconnect it from the outlet. Call the repairman.

Fire: a fire in an appliance usually means there is a defect in the wiring, and there is danger of getting a severe shock. The first thing to do is pull the main house switch. *Then call the fire department.* If you can safely reach the plug, disconnect the appliance, and attempt to put out or control the flames with a dry chemical or carbon dioxide extinguisher. Never use water. Do not try to smother the blaze with a blanket or rug until you have been able to pull the plug from the electrical outlet.

Electric Shock: should you receive a shock from any appliance, large or small, immediately disconnect it from the outlet by pulling the plug. Don't attempt to switch it off. Either put the appliance away, or put a sign on it so that no one else will use it.

How to Tackle Dishwasher Problems

Symptom	Possible Cause and Action
Machine starts, but does not wash	Outlet strainer clogged. Remove and clean with soft brush Jammed spray arms. Make sure that dishes or utensils are not obstructing spray arm's path of rotation
Noisy operation	Dishes not placed securely in racks, or dislodged by water action Machine not level or on solid footing. Adjust leveling screws
Failure to dry dishes	Wrong water temperature. Set water heater thermostat at 150 degrees Machine set for wrong cycle Machine overloaded, or dishes nested Heating element not working. Call for service
Dishes are not washed clean	Use recommended detergent in specified amounts Improper loading. Follow manual for loading instructions Dishes improperly or incompletely precleaned Low water temperature. Adjust thermostat on hot water heater to higher setting Insufficient water. Unclog water inlets Clogged fill-valve strainer. Follow manual for cleaning instructions Detergent dispenser does not open. Clean and check it to be certain catch is not broken or bent Machine controls improperly set. Be sure to choose correct cycle
Machine won't fill or operate	Door or lid not closed and latched Lack of power. Fuse may have blown or circuit breaker may have tripped Check controls. Are buttons pressed, and/or dials properly set? If the dishwasher is a so-called portable type, the water may be turned off
Not enough water	Low water pressure. May be caused by water being run for other purposes while dishwasher is operating. If this is not the case, call for service. Check water pressure at faucets. Check water inlet

Washing Machine Troubleshooting

Symptoms	Possible Cause and Action
Failure to start	Door or lid not closed and latched. This is a frequent problem with front loading machines Cycle control dials or buttons not correctly set. Check and set for cycle you want Water supply shutoff valves closed. Open them. (To take water pressure off the washer's valves, keep these shutoff valves closed when the washer is not in use)
Water does not flow into machine	Cycle buttons or dials not set Door or lid not fully closed Water supply valves closed Kinks in hoses; loose wiring in machine; screen of washer inlet valve clogged
Water too hot or too cold	Temperature and cycle controls not set properly One of the water supply shutoff valves closed Water supply hoses attached to the wrong inlets—hot to cold and cold to hot Hot water heater not operating properly. See chapter 6
Failure to spin, or washer stops during the spin	Door or lid not fully closed Many washers will stop if the load is unbalanced, or does not spin evenly. Rearrange load properly, and restart machine at spin cycle
Machine vibrates	Machine not correctly leveled. Check with spirit level, and adjust leveling legs Wash load not properly balanced
Failure to drain	Clogged drain or kinks in drain hose. Disconnect and check Excessive suds. Add cold water, and start cycle to dissolve. Run briefly, and drain

Emergency Steps for Range and Over

Symptoms	Possible Cause and Action
Failure to bake evenly	Oven not properly leveled. Check with spirit level; shim if necessary
	Thermostat set incorrectly. Call for service
	Using a utensil that is not the correct size or shape
	Poor circulation of heat caused by using utensils too big for the oven
	Placing utensil in the wrong position—too close to bottom, sides, or top
	Too many utensils used at same time
Failure of appliance outlet on the range	Timing controls set incorrectly
	Defect in the appliance itself. To check it, try it in another outlet
	Blown fuse or tripped circuit breaker
Poor results from a burner or a surface unit controlled by a thermostat	Using a utensil that cannot conduct heat evenly
	Improper setting of thermostat
	Fouled sensing device. Cleaning required to correct it

Clothes Dryer Won't Dry? Try...

Symptoms	Possible Cause and Action
Failure to start	Door or lid not fully closed
	Controls set incorrectly. Make certain that dials are properly set, and buttons fully pushed down
	Motor overheated. Machine may have motor-overload protector. Let motor cool a few minutes before trying to start dryer again
Clothes do not dry, or they take too long to dry	Controls set incorrectly
	Machine overloaded
	Clogged lint filter; remove and clean
	Dryer load too wet when put into machine
	Vent pipe may be partially clogged, or vent trap may be stuck. Release it
	If the dryer is gas operated, gas may be turned off. Pilot light may be out. Check valves, check other appliances to see if service has been interrupted

Refrigerator and Freezer Fixit Tips

Symptoms	Possible Cause and Action
Excessive noise or vibration	Loose shelves or improper storage; check and alter
	Unit is not level. Adjust leveling screws
	Drip pan may need defrosting; try this
	Evaporator out of position; correct it
Starts with a groan	Dust and dirt on the motor. Unplug unit, and clean with vacuum cleaner
	Motor needs oiling. Check manual
Frequent and long cycling	Door opened too often, and kept open too long
	Rubber door gasket does not seal. Try cleaning with soap and water; if cleaning does not help, call for service
	Malfunction of door latch. Use Fixit Rule 2. Call for service
	Weather unusually hot and humid
	Thermostat set too low
	Faulty interior light switch on door may cause light to stay lit with door closed. This produces considerable heat. Unscrew bulb
	Coils behind unit coated with dust or grime. Vacuum clean after disconnecting
Excessive frost in freezer compartment	See above for cause of frequent and lengthy cycling. Same condition may let in excess moisture, causing frost to accumulate in freezer compartments
	Automatic defroster out of order. If all other causes ruled out, call for service
	If unit does not defrost automatically, it may need to be defrosted
	Freezer compartment door left open too long
	Freezer compartment door does not shut tightly. Use Rule 2. Call for service
Frozen foods thaw in freezing compartment	Malfunction of automatic defrosting system
	If unit does not defrost automatically, it may need to be defrosted
	Dust or grime on coils. See above
	Thermostat set too high
	Thermostat turned off or not working. If the latter, call for service

Heating and Hot Water Hints

6

There's nothing like plenty of heat and hot water. If you have too little for comfort—or none at all because of a breakdown—there are things you can do before calling for outside help.

When it comes to heat, I like plenty of it. Among the great pleasures of my life, I include gently boiling myself to a delicate lobster pink in a tub of hot, hot water.

Fortunately, heating systems are not great sources of trouble. Unfortunately, when trouble does arise, repairs and major adjustments usually call for a professional heating serviceman. Yet, before you call for service, there are a number of things you can and should do for yourself to keep the home fires burning, and, in these days of rising prices and energy crises, to get the most value from your heating dollar.

Most modern homes are equipped with one of three types of furnaces: oil, gas, or electric. No matter which of the three you have in your home, electricity plays a key role in its operation. In an emergency the furnace can be turned off by the switch controlling its electrical power. You should know where it is.

In most homes the furnace control switch is located in the furnace room or utility room, or on a wall near the furnace.

Besides this switch there is—or should be—a fuse or circuit breaker in the entry box to protect the circuit the furnace is on. You will find it when you study the house circuits as I suggested in Chapter 5.

If the furnace is not operating as you think it should the place to begin your troubleshooting is with the thermostat.

Thermostat Problems

In addition to the fuse (or circuit breaker) and furnace switch, there is another crucial on-off point in most of today's heating plants, the thermostat. Thermostats are simply switches that respond to temperature changes

Left: the thermostat is the key to your heating system. Don't try to adjust it, but do clean it periodically with a paintbrush or syringe.

Right: when the heating season begins, bleed the air from the radiators. This will improve their heating efficiency, and also eliminate annoying noise as they warm up.

to start the furnace, or shut it off. They are precision instruments, and the only maintenance you should provide is to remove accumulated dust and lint from under the cover. This can be done by taking off the cover, and blowing out the dust (a small rubber ear syringe works well), or by careful, very light brushing with a watercolor or small paintbrush.

Thermostats merely control room temperature. The amount of fuel the furnace burns is constant when it is on. Turning the thermostat up to a higher-than-normal setting will not heat the house faster than turning it just to the temperature desired. If your house does not heat well, or you feel that, in comparison with other houses of the same size, your heating bills are higher than they should be, check the thermostat. For maximum efficiency, thermostats should always be located about five feet up from the floor on an inside wall, away from drafts and direct sources of heat. They should never be near an outside door or window. Don't camouflage the thermostat, or hide it behind doors, furniture, or drapes. Remember also that even the heat from a nearby lamp or television set will throw it off.

If the thermostat in your house is much more than six or seven years old, have it inspected by a serviceman to make certain that it is still operating efficiently. If he advises you that your thermostat isn't located properly, you should have a new one installed in a location that he suggests. This will call for an expense of up to $50 and, possibly, a wall repair (see Chapter 8). Still, the investment will pay for itself many times over in terms of comfort, and in dollars saved on fuel bills if you pay for your own.

Keeping the Heating System in Good Condition

1. *Motors.* Most furnaces have one or more

Vacuum between radiator
vanes for better heating.

motors. Oil burner motors and blower motors on hot air systems should be lubricated at least two or three times a year. The motors and pumps of circulating hot water systems also need regular oiling.

2. *Filters, Vents, and Radiators.* Hot air heating systems usually have filters in the furnace, or ducts to trap dust and lint. Check these at least two or three times a year. If you can't see light through a filter when you hold it up to a window or other source of light, it's time for a new one.

If yours is a hot water system, bleed (drain) the vents on the radiators at the beginning of each heating season to release trapped air. This lets heated water flow freely to give you more heat, and also prevents banging noises as the radiators warm up. Start with the highest radiator, or the one farthest from the

furnace. Drain off a cup or two of water from each one.

Dust and lint between the fins and openings in radiator covers and grills can cut down on radiator efficiency. To make certain that the radiators are putting out all their heat, you should clean them with the vacuum as a regular routine.

If you have a gas furnace, it's a good idea to keep the pilot light on in summer. This will keep your heating equipment dry during the humid weather, and so reduce the possibility of rust and corrosion inside.

3. *Annual Checkup.* At the beginning of each heating season, it is worth the $15 or $20 fee to have your heating system cleaned and serviced by a heating service specialist. This service is usually provided by either the utility company, if you heat with gas or

When your furnace or hot water heater is giving you trouble, your first thought does not have to be to call for professional help. Sometimes you may be able to solve the problem yourself by using a few of the simple tactics these charts list.

First Aid for Furnace Failures

Problem	Possible Cause	What to try
Furnace doesn't run (all types)	Thermostat may have been turned very low	Turn dial to highest setting
	Thermostat contact points may be dirty	Clean contact points
	Main switch may have been turned off accidentally	Check; turn on if necessary
	Fuse may have blown, or circuit breaker may have tripped off	Change fuse, or switch circuit breaker on, as needed
	Burner's pilot light may have gone out (gas only)	Relight pilot light; follow directions on equipment if available; if not, do this: 1. Turn thermostat to lowest setting 2. Shut gas supply valve (not main house valve) 3. Wait 5 mins., then turn on pilot light valve 4. Light pilot with match (If your furnace has a button instead of valve, hold it down while you light pilot, and keep it down until pilot flame has been burning at least a full minute) 5. When pilot light burns well, turn on main furnace valve
Escaping gas smell (gas furnace)		Shut off entire gas supply at main house supply valve at once, and call gas company
New fuse blows after replacement, or circuit breaker trips off again after being switched to on position		Leave power off, and call for service

When Hot Water Heaters Don't Work

Type of heater	Problem	Possible Cause	Possible Cure
Gas	No hot water	Pilot light is out	Relight; if no instructions on heater, follow steps in chart on furnaces
		Gas supply valve is closed	Open fully; the handle should run parallel to pipe
		Thermostat turned down or off	If thermostat switch is not buried in the insulation, turn it full on; otherwise, call for service
	Not enough hot water	Thermostat may be set too low	Normal setting is 140 degrees. Reset if you can get to it
		Gas supply valve may be partially closed	Make sure it's fully open
	Water too hot	Thermostat may be set too high	Reset to 140 degrees if you can
	Steam or boiling water coming out	Thermostat has failed	Shut down heater, but not water inlet; call for service
Electric	No hot water	Switch may be off	Turn it on
		Fuse may have blown, or circuit breaker tripped off	Replace fuse, or switch circuit breaker on
	Not enough hot water	Thermostat may not be working	Call for service
		Heating element may have failed	Call for service
	Water scalding	Same as above	Same as above
All types	Leaking relief valve	Tendency to leak	Catch water in container; if leak is constant and heavy, call for service

Note: the problem with your hot water heater may be that it's just too small for your family's needs—remember, a hot bath or long shower may take 15 or 20 gallons, and a big wash 30 to 35 gallons of the supply. Two possible answers to this problem is to do some scheduling, or to get a bigger heater. If you have a new heater, or if you have regularly drained the tank in the past, it's a good idea to drain dirt and rust out every three to six months. (There's a faucet near the bottom of the tank for this purpose.) If you have never drained the tank, however, and it is old, don't start draining now.

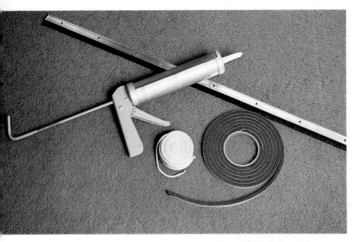

is set, check the burner cutoff control. If you cannot find and correct the trouble, call for service.

Another indication of overheating that you should take warning from is hot water backing up in the cold water supply pipe.

Emergency Procedures
There are going to be unavoidable times when things don't go right. For such an emergency, it isn't always necessary to call for help, because there are some steps you can take to correct the situation yourself. See

Your house will retain heat better in the winter, and stay cooler in the summer if you have it properly insulated. Above: among the easy-to-install insulating materials are caulking (in gun) for outside of windows and door frames, aluminum stripping for doors, felt for the inside of window and door frames, and plastic caulking for any kind of a crack anywhere at all. Right: aluminum weatherstrip for bottom of door must be installed so that it doesn't hit door jamb.

Above: if the aluminum weatherstrip doesn't fit width of door, cut it to size with a hacksaw.

Right: screw strip to inside of door so that felt strip fits tight against the door sill.

electricity, or by a service representative from the fuel oil company, if oil is your fuel. Besides getting all systems in a "go" condition, the inspection has the added advantage that, should problems develop later on, the serviceman will come without question—and he will know something about the peculiarities of your furnace.

Hot Water Tank Rumbles
If your hot water tank makes rumbling noises, it may be a sign of overheating. This, in turn, could lead to the development of explosive pressure. So, shut off the burner immediately. Be sure that the pressure relief valve is working, and then check the temperature of the water at the nearest outlet with a thermometer. If the temperature is above that for which the tank's thermostat

the charts on pages 82–83 for things you can do in a heating or hot water emergency.

Weatherproofing and Insulation
The time to start thinking of ways to keep your home warm and cozy is before winter begins. Besides the steps you take to get the furnace in good operating condition, consider the extent of heat loss through ill-fitting storm sashes, uninsulated walls, attic, or floor, and cracks around windows and doors. These heat wasters account for a substantial portion of your fuel bills—sometimes as much as 25 per cent, heating specialists say.

Taking steps to see that your house is adequately protected against heat loss in winter is also a very good way to ensure your comfort in hot weather. If your home or any portion of it is artificially air-conditioned, the same methods you use to keep cold air out will also help to retain that expensively produced cool air during the summer.

Depending on the materials you select, any woman who can hammer a nail or drive a screw can handle most of the work involved in weatherproofing cheaply and quickly.

Weatherstripping to prevent drafts from entering around windows and doors is available in a variety of easy-to-apply, flexible materials including felt stripping, foam rubber with a piece of adhesive backing, vinyl tubular gasket, and vinyl-covered

Above: weatherstrip sides of doors with adhesive-backed or tack-on materials of felt or rubber to make a tight seal when the door is closed. You can also use these on the inside of window frames.

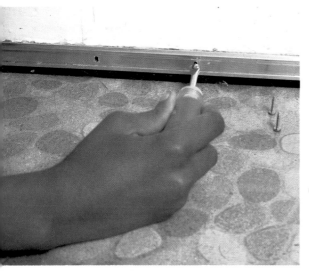

sponge. These are particularly useful for windows. For the bottom of doors you will want rigid stripping made of strips of wood or metal to which are fastened flexible rubber strips or sponge backing. The simplest to install of all these is a metal or aluminum strip with a felt or vinyl sweep that is screwed to the bottom of the door on the inside.

Generally the flexible types of weather-stripping are the best choice for the do-it-yourselfer. Which material you select depends on how much you want to spend, and how long you expect the stripping to last. The felt types are the shortest lived of the lot—two seasons at best. Vinyl stripping is more attractive, and wears longer. Adhesive-backed foam rubber does not last a long time, but it may be your only choice for aluminum windows on which you wish to avoid nailing.

The spring metal stripping is the most expensive, but it also is permanent—and therefore, in the long run, the cheapest.

When you get around to weatherstripping the frames of windows and doors, I strongly recommend flexible weatherstripping as fast and easy to install. You can cut most types with scissors and fasten them with tacks, brads, or staples. For this purpose there is no tool handier than a hand operated staple gun. No matter what types of weatherstripping you choose, it should be fastened so that the flexible, or contact edge, presses snugly against a face of the closed window or door. Nail or staple it every four or five inches, and at every corner. Cut the weatherstripping for the window frames into three pieces, two to go around each sash, and a shorter length to fit where the two sashes meet. Install each

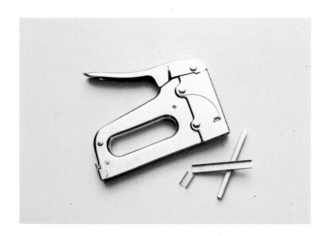

The hand operated staple gun is a luxury tool, but it has a thousand-and-one uses for the home handywoman. With it you can install weatherstripping rapidly and securely with minimum effort.

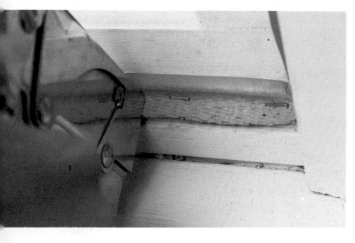

Above: installing felt weatherstripping around a window frame. Felt as an insulating material has a short life, lasting only about two years. Below: a more satisfactory form of weatherstripping is made of plastic with a sponge rubber core. It makes a better seal, and has a longer life.

sash section in one continuous strip, stapling it to the window stops on the sides; staple the upper and lower section to the sill and frame. Tack the shorter piece along the top of the lower sash so that it presses against the upper sash. You may find it necessary to cut this piece into two short sections to fit around the sash lock.

On doors, fasten the weatherstripping in one piece around the stops. Its placement on the stops depends on the type of stripping you use. Apply the felt and foam types to the inside face of the stops. Vinyl tubular stripping should be tacked to the side of the stop so that it presses evenly against the face of the door.

Wooden casement windows can be weatherstripped in a similar fashion, with the stripping fastened to the stops. Use channel stripping of the vinyl variety for steel windows.

Weatherstripping accomplishes a great deal, but it is not always enough, particularly in older homes. There are other potential problem areas.

While your attention is on the problems of draft control, why not inspect the condition of the putty in all window sashes. If you find it cracked or broken, the putty should be patched or replaced. Follow the procedure outlined in replacing a broken window pane.

Check the bottom of the window sills where they meet the wall. Settling of the foundation can create a leak point at this spot. If you find a separation between sill and wall, cover it with quarter-round molding.

On the outside, check for cracks between the window, and the siding and sill; apply caulking compound as necessary. One particularly vulnerable spot on concrete or brick sills is the joint between sill and window frame. This joint should be caulked or painted over with a coating of asphalt compound.

Storm windows of any type, of course, should fit snugly into the window frames, or they are virtually useless.

Uninsulated wood floors over crawl spaces can admit cold air through cracks in the flooring, or because of gaps under the

Left: caulking cracks and openings makes the house more comfortable by keeping heat in and drafts out. This pays dollar dividends by saving on heating bills. Easiest caulking to use is this putty-like one.

Below: heat loss occurs around joints between house siding and door and window frames. They should be permanently caulked. Use a caulking gun for a faster, neater, and easier job.

molding at the bottom of baseboards. Also look for gaps under the door sills.

Your winterizing inspection should not omit the outside walls and roofing. Check for loose or broken siding, and for cracks or breaks in masonry. Roofs should be inspected, and potential leak points repaired. The condition of flashing at roof-to-wall seams, and around windows, is of particular importance. Then turn your attention to the condition of your home's insulation, and the installation of heat-retaining materials where they are needed most.

Making Doors and Windows Work

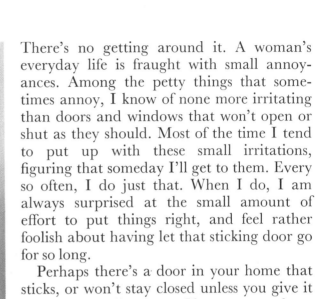

7

When doors and windows are balky, you can easily fix them. The woman on the left, trying to open a stuck door with a hard tug, is using the least effective way. The woman above will get farther. She's taking direct action by using a simple tool to pry open a window that was painted tightly shut.

There's no getting around it. A woman's everyday life is fraught with small annoyances. Among the petty things that sometimes annoy, I know of none more irritating than doors and windows that won't open or shut as they should. Most of the time I tend to put up with these small irritations, figuring that someday I'll get to them. Every so often, I do just that. When I do, I am always surprised at the small amount of effort to put things right, and feel rather foolish about having let that sticking door go for so long.

Perhaps there's a door in your home that sticks, or won't stay closed unless you give it a window-rattling bang. If so, you may have put off fixing it, fearing that the job would call for some major operation, such as planing the top or bottom, or doing some carpentry on the frame. Both carpentry on the frame and planing the door are last resort applications, because the treatment of acute and chronic stickitis of doors is a simple procedure, calling only for the tools in your Homeowner's Survival Kit.

Doors that Stick

Before looking for other sources of trouble, open the door wide enough to expose the hinge screws, then try each of them with a screwdriver. Tighten any that are loose, because even the tiniest amount of play will let the door sag enough to rub or bind in one corner. If the old screws have chewed up the wood so badly that you can no longer tighten them satisfactorily remove them entirely, and fill the holes by hammering in wooden match sticks or wooden plugs that have been dipped into glue. Trim the ends off the matches or

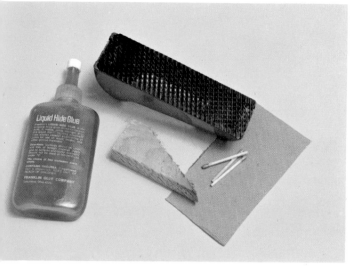

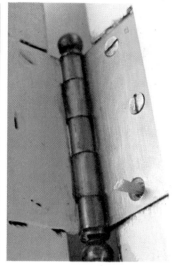

For repairs and first-aid to sticking doors, you will need the basic tools of hammer and screwdriver, plus others such as glue, small pieces of cardboard, a wedge or two, wooden matches, and a tool called a rasp for taking off excess wood.

When screws won't hold, fill old screw holes with matches or a wooden plug soaked in glue, and trim off the excess.

Before starting work on a sticking door, locate the place that binds by running some cardboard between door and frame.

plug flush with the frame, and reinsert the original screws.

If all the hinge screws are tight, your next step is to locate the exact spot where the door binds. Shut the door, and run a sheet of thin cardboard around the edges. Wherever it binds, the door is rubbing. In most cases this will be near the top or bottom corners along the outside edge.

Door Sticks at Bottom

The problem probably is that the bottom hinge is set too deeply into the door jamb, or frame. The simplest corrective procedure is to *shim* out the bottom hinge by inserting one or more thicknesses of cardboard behind the lower hinge leaf. This will push the lower part of the door slightly out from the door jamb, raising it sufficiently to keep the bottom from rubbing. To install a cardboard shim, you will have to unscrew the hinge leaf when the door is open, and propped up underneath. You can cut triangular blocks of wood for props, or use several magazines, or a book.

The next step is to cut a piece of cardboard slightly smaller than the hinge leaf, and slip it behind the hinge. Then screw the hinge back

When you remove hinge screws, the door will sag unless you prop it up with wedges, newspapers, or magazines.

Left: shimming alone will not always cure sticking doors. Sanding may be needed, too.

Right: door that won't catch may be corrected by placing a shim beneath the strike plate.

Below: cut shims for hinges or face plates just slightly smaller than the metal parts.

To separate hinge, you have to remove pin joining the two parts. Use screwdriver and hammer, tapping gently.

Next remove leaf of hinge that's fastened to frame. Scrape old paint out of screw heads if necessary.

Place cardboard shim cut to correct size under hinge leaf, and replace screws. Plug holes if you need to.

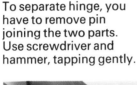

in place, filling the holes to make the screws hold if necessary. When more clearance is needed, use another shim on top of the first one. If the door still sticks near the bottom, you may have to trim off a small amount of wood at the point where rubbing occurs. This can be done most easily by using a sheet of coarse sandpaper wrapped around a block of wood.

Door Sticks Along Top Outside Corner

The cause of this is the top hinge. Try shimming it out.

Door Doesn't Close

Shimming out the hinges is also the remedy to try on doors that have the nasty habit of springing open if you don't slam them hard. Use narrow cardboard shims, about half the width of the hinge leaf, inserted under the back half of the hinge leaf only, near the pin. This tends to tilt the hinges more into the door opening, swinging the whole door around so that it can close more freely without binding. The procedure is the same as described above, except that you slip the strips of cardboard under the back edges of both hinges, top and bottom.

Right: when windows
have been painted shut,
try breaking the paint
seal with putty knife.

Door Will Not Stay Closed

The most likely cause of this problem is that
the latch bolt does not engage the strike plate
opening. A close look will usually reveal that
the opening in the strike plate on the door
jamb is not properly lined up with the latch
bolt. Try curing this condition by moving the
strike plate so that is is a fraction of an inch
higher or lower on the door frame. Another
way to accomplish the same thing is to take
the plate off, and file the opening slightly
larger at the top or bottom. If the strike plate
is recessed too deeply into the door jamb, or
if the door itself has shrunk (or has been
planed too much) so that the latch bolt no
longer reaches into the strike plate opening,
the plate can be moved closer to the door edge
by shimming out behind it with one or more
thicknesses of cardboard.

Window Troubles

When wooden windows stick or bind, the
trouble is usually caused either by dampness
that may result in swelling, or by someone
who has carelessly slapped on paint that has
hardened around the edges of the sash and
frame.

To open windows that are stuck shut
because of hardened paint, try breaking the
seal by forcing a putty knife between the
edge of the sash and the top molding. While
you tap the blade in, twist the handle
slightly. Pry along both sides of the sash, and
along the bottom of the sill, till the sash can
be raised. This is bound to chip the paint. So
you have to make a choice between a
permanently closed window, a little chipped
paint, or a further fixit job that will take care
of the chipped paint, too.

Left: use hatchet as both wedge and lever on outside of window, and exert pressure evenly.

Above: use a wood block and hammer to drive the sash away from the stop molding in order to free moisture-swollen windows, or to drive stop molding tight against the sash to eliminate drafts.

In severe cases, you may have to pry the window open from the bottom with a heavy tool. A scout ax is ideal, *but work from the outside* to avoid damaging the interior trim. Tap the ax gently between the bottom of the sash and sill. Edge it along the full width of the window, lifting gently each time until the sash breaks free. If you go at this carefully, neither the sill nor the sash will be marred or damaged.

Once you've gotten the window open, use a sharp tool to scrape off the paint from the outside edge of the stop molding where it rubs against the inside face of the sash. Scrape carefully to avoid chipping or gouging the wood, then smooth with a piece of fine sandpaper wrapped around a small block of wood. Also check the outer edge of the window sill to see whether the bottom of the sash is rubbing at this point.

If the windows stick because the wood has swollen from absorbed moisture you may be able to solve the problem by using a wooden block and a hammer. Place the block against the wood of the sash, and smack it sharply with the hammer, working it up and down the full length, and on both sides of the molding and sash.

Windows that are merely hard to open rather than stuck can often be cured by simple lubrication. Rub the inside of the tracks with a paraffin block, or the end of a candle. You can also use any of the many special grease sticks and aerosol lubricants for this purpose. They work particularly well on windows that have built-in metal weatherstripping in the channels. It helps to clean the metal beforehand by rubbing it firmly with fine steel wool.

Casement windows are not without their

troubles. Those that hinge at the sides may be extremely hard to open or close even with a lot of huffing and puffing. If you can't close them, this not only permits cold drafts to chill you, but can also result in a considerable loss of heat in the wintertime.

The most common offender on steel-framed casement windows is rust around the hinges and along the edges. Periodic painting with a good quality exterior trim paint or enamel prevents this, particularly if you apply a coat of rust-resistant primer before you put on the new trim coat.

Before you paint a steel window, check the condition of the putty, or glazing compound, around the outside of the glass. It's no great trick to scrape out old, cracked putty, and replace it with new. Before laying the putty in, give the bare metal a coat or two of rust-resistant primer. Painting and puttying, fortunately, are not annual operations. You should, however, lubricate casement windows at least once a year to keep all parts operating smoothly. Apply a few drops of oil to each

hinge, making certain that the oil penetrates into the space between the hinge leaves, as well as to the pin that joins the two halves together.

Most steel casement windows are opened and closed from the inside by a crank that pushes out a lever to open the sash. The window end of this lever slides in a grooved track to swing the sash open or closed. This bit of metal benefits from a periodic scraping with a wire brush to clear out accumulated rust, dirt, and old grease. Then apply a liberal shot of new oil or light grease to the groove. An aerosol-type lubricating spray can also be used, though the track should still be cleaned well before this is applied.

A few drops of oil in the joint where the handle enters the case helps to keep it operating smoothly. If a handle should not work, remove it by unscrewing the two bolts at each side. Wash out the old hardened lubricant with kerosene, or simply scrape it out with a wire brush and plenty of hot water and household cleaner. Then apply fresh

94

Above: use a wire brush to remove rust and dirt from casement windows.

Left: windows that bind can benefit from an application of candle wax.

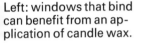

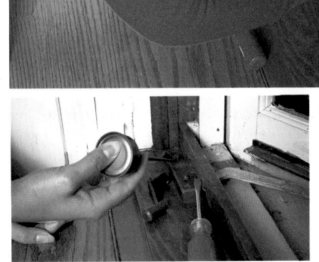

Above: a few drops of oil applied to a clean track will prevent rusting, and also help make operation easy.

Right: lubrication of the crank mechanism of casement windows once a year helps keep them in good working order.

grease of the white or nonstaining type. If the gears are worn so badly that they no longer mesh properly, the entire handle should be replaced.

Aluminum windows—casement or sliding —do not need painting for protection, though there is no reason not to paint them for decorative purposes if you want to do so. Aluminum, however, is subject to pitting— particularly if your house is located near the seashore. An occasional coat of car wax will help to keep the metal looking shiny. If your aluminum windows are already pitted, a vigorous going over with fine steel wool before applying the wax will do wonders. Don't forget to apply wax to all edges, and inside the tracks as well. On sliding windows, clean out the grooves at least once a year to keep them operating smoothly.

Storm Damage on Windows

When a window breaks during a storm, it is often impractical or impossible to repair it at once. As a stopgap measure, staple a large piece of plastic sheet to the casement, sides, and sills. Clear plastic should be a part of every homeowner's emergency repair supply, but if you have been caught short, cover the

Think that replacing
a broken window pane
is one job you don't
want to tackle? You'll
find that it's not so
hard if you follow these
steps and work carefully.

window with any material that will keep out the elements—plywood, hardboard, or even an old blanket.

After your emergency measure has served its purpose, repairing the window comes next.

Replacing a Broken Window Pane

The job of replacing a broken pane of glass in windows or storm sash is a home repair project you can handle while the sash remains in its frame; you will, however, find the job easier if the sash can be removed and laid out flat.

Above: pull out all the broken pieces of glass.
Below: now clean out the bulk of the old putty.

1. Wear work gloves to remove the broken glass by gently pulling the pieces out in as large sections as possible. If a piece is held tight by the hardened putty, rock it carefully back and forth to break the bond, then pull straight out. Have a cardboard box handy so you can dispose of the broken pieces of glass without further handling. Stubborn chips embedded in corners can be knocked out by hitting gently with hammer and putty knife.
2. After you have removed the broken glass, scrape out all of the old, hardened putty with your knife or screwdriver. While you are removing the old putty, pull out the bits of flat triangular metal (glazier's points) either by pulling them out with your pliers, or by prying them out.
3. After you have removed all the old putty and glazier's points, scrape the groove clean, and then paint it with a coat of boiled linseed oil, or thinned house paint. This is an important step that should not be skipped, for it keeps the wood from absorbing too much oil from the new glazing compound you are soon going to put in the groove, and will help the compound stick better and stay

Above: use pliers to remove old glazier's points.
Below: clean out the remaining bits of old putty.

Above: use a sharp tool to clean out the channel.
Below: carefully measure opening for a new pane.

Paint the groove with a coat of boiled linseed oil or thinned house paint. This keeps the wood from absorbing oil from new putty or glazing compound.

Next, lay a thin layer of putty or glazing compound in the groove as a bed for the new pane. This step is optional, but helps improve the seal.

pliable longer. Such care always pays off.

4. Measure the opening, and have your dealer cut a new pane. Be sure to order it about $\frac{1}{8}$ inch smaller than the actual size of the opening in length and width. This will give a $\frac{1}{16}$ inch leeway on all sides, making it easier to slip the new pane into place. If you are replacing one pane in a multiple paned sash, buy single strength glass. Larger panes require double strength glass. Also buy a small can of glazing compound, and a small package of glazier's points.

5. Before placing the new pane in the sash groove, lay in a thin bed of putty or glazing compound. I've found that many professional glaziers omit this step, but, as for me, I always follow traditional methods—hoping, I guess, that a little extra produces a better job. The option is yours on this one. Still, the bed of glazing material does help cushion the

glass against shock or uneven stress, and decreases the danger of leakage around the edges of the pane.

6. Press the glass gently but firmly into its cushion of putty, then fasten it securely in position by driving glazier's points into the frame around all four sides. These can be driven in by laying the side of a screwdriver against the point, and tapping the top of the screwdriver gently with a hammer. Some points are designed with a little edge against which the screwdriver will fit. Use two points along each side on panes up to two feet. Larger panes need three to four points on each side. Remember it is these points that hold the glass in place, and not the putty or glazing compound.

7. One way to apply the final layer of glazing compound to seal the new pane into place is to roll strips about the thickness of a pencil,

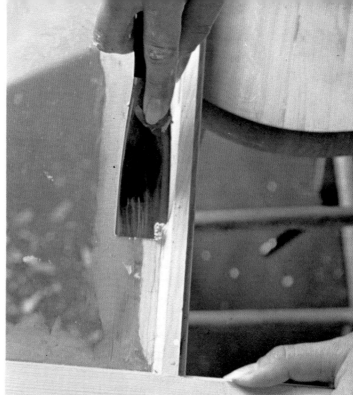

Place new pane on bed of putty, and press down firmly. Then insert new glazier's points, using at least two points along each side of the pane.

Right: use putty knife to lift off excess putty. Let putty smudges dry out for a day or two, then use turpentine-moistened rag to clean them off.

Apply a final layer of putty or glazing compound with a putty knife, and shape it to form a bevel that slopes smoothly from the sash to the glass.

and lay them into the groove around the edge of the sash. I've never been able to do this with any great success, so I prefer to apply the glazing compound directly with the putty knife.

Either way, use a putty knife to press the glazing material firmly into position. Shape it to form a smooth beveled edge sloping from the sash to the glass. Put on enough glazing compound so that the finished level comes high enough on the glass to match the level of the molding on the inside. Putty smudges on the glass can be removed by wiping with a rag moistened with turpentine, after the putty has been allowed to dry for a day or two. After a week or two you can paint the compound to match the trim of your house. Let the paint run slightly beyond the edge, and onto the glass, to assure a weather-tight seal.

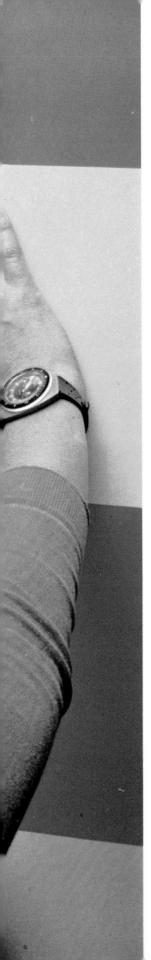

Simple Solutions for Floors and Walls

8

One of the easiest of all home fixit tasks is replacing a damaged floor tile. The hardest part of the job may be to find a tile that matches the ones you have.

Because walls and floors don't do much of anything but stand or lie there, you would think that nothing would ever go wrong with them. Anyone who has lived in an apartment or house for any length of time, however, knows better. All manner of things can go wrong. Walls develop cracks, or the installation of something leaves a hole. Wooden floors develop squeaks, and eventually need sanding.

While elaborate wall or floor repairs should be left to professionals, there are a number of small repairs that can be handled by the fixit devotee.

Patching Cracks and Holes in Wallboard and Plaster

Wallboard and plaster are made of the same material, so the supplies for, and techniques of patching are similar. Actually, wallboard —sometimes called plasterboard or gypsumboard—is a layer of plaster sandwiched between two sheets of heavy paper or cardboard. It is simply nailed to studs. Plaster, which is applied wet, is bound to a wall by wooden or metal laths that have been nailed to the studs. The first layer of plaster is forced between and around the laths to form the bond. Subsequent layers build the wall up to the desired surface level. In newer buildings, plaster may be applied to smooth wallboard panels that have been treated with an adhesive.

Cracks in both wallboard and plaster can be patched with spackle, a patented crack patcher, or a caulk. Before applying the material you should wirebrush narrow cracks. When patching wider, deeper cracks, clean out all loose crumbling material with a can

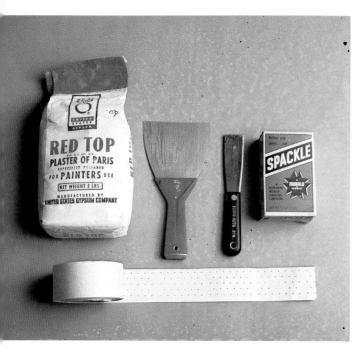

While repairing plaster and gypsumboard walls is not the easiest of fixit jobs, you can certainly do it. Materials needed include patching plaster, spackle and spackling tape, and plastering tools.

First step in repairing cracks is to clean out all loose plaster and dust with a sharp tool.

To prevent patch from drying out too quickly, dampen the crack and the surface around it.

opener or screwdriver to make a firm surface. A firmer bond results if you undercut the edges.

Before applying the patching material, you should dampen the edges of the crack so moisture is not drawn out of the patch, unless, that is, the instructions on the patching material tell you not to. Fill a deep crack with two layers of patch. The first should come almost to the surface, to be followed with a thin finish coat that feathers out—that is, reduces the edges—an inch or two on either side of the crack.

It is common for nails to come through gypsumboard walls as new walls begin to dry and settle. This is called "nail pop", and it is not difficult to fix. First drive the popped nail flush to the wall with your nail set. Then drive the nail again, this time making it go slightly below the surface so that the resulting indentation, or "dimple", will hold new plaster. Fill the dimple with patching plaster or compound, smooth with a putty knife, and sand even after letting dry for 24 hours, or longer if you have the patience to wait.

Another problem with gypsumboard walls can arise if the tape lifts. This happens in the same area as nail popping, and is also easy to repair. First, trim the tape at the top and bottom of the damaged spot, making sure you get it perfectly straight. Next, pull the tape gently upward until you reach a spot where the bond is firm. Trim the tape off at that point. Now, put on a layer of patching compound, over which you lay a new piece of tape cut exactly to fit the space. Cover the tape with more patching compound, let dry, and sand smooth.

Holes in gypsumboard are usually without backing. If a hole is very large, it will likely meet a stud. In this case, cut a piece of gypsumboard to fit the trimmed up hole, nail it to the stud, then tape and spackle the seams as if you were installing a wall from scratch.

Holes or wide cracks that go all the way to the lath in plaster walls or wallboard require more extensive treatment. Here is the method you will have to use.

1. Knock out all loose, cracked plaster with

After mixing patching plaster or compound, work it into the crack, and smooth it carefully.

Allow the patch to dry completely—about 24 hours or so—and finish by sandpapering.

Dry wall construction is the most common type in homes. In it, gypsumboard panels are nailed to studs, the joints are covered with tape, and the whole is covered with spackle or joint compound to produce an invisible seam (left). A rarer type uses specially treated gypsumboard as a lath for a plaster surface (center). Traditional plaster walls are made of metal or wood lath nailed to studs, bonded by a first layer of plaster. Successive plaster layers are then built up (right).

hammer and chisel. Take care not to cause further cracking. Undercut the edges to strengthen the eventual bond.

2. Check the lath for damage or excessive moisture that could be decomposing the plaster. If you encounter signs of substantial damage at this point, it may be advisable to call in a professional.

3. Having assured yourself of the good condition of the backing material, prepare a batch of patching plaster following the package instructions.

4. Using a sponge, dampen the area surrounding the patch. Dry plaster will absorb water from the patching material, weakening and shrinking it.

5. If the patch is smaller than four inches square, fill and surface it with one application of the patching plaster.

6. Larger holes may require three layers of plaster. The first one should fill a little more than half the depth. Before it dries, score it with a nail to provide "tooth" for the succeeding layer. The second layer, applied after the first has dried (about four hours), requires a rewetting of the patch area. This coat should come within $\frac{1}{2}$ to $\frac{1}{4}$ inch of the surface. The third coat is applied as soon as the second has dried. Remember to moisten the patch area yet again to prevent shrinkage. This coat has to be textured to match the rest of the wall.

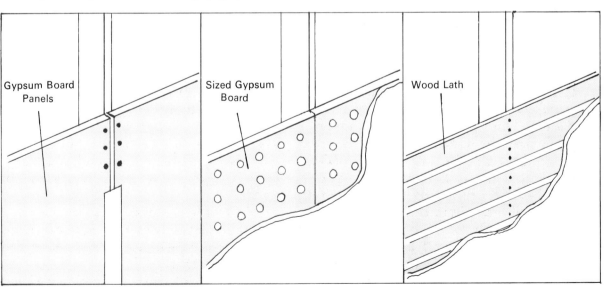

Gypsum Board Panels

Sized Gypsum Board

Wood Lath

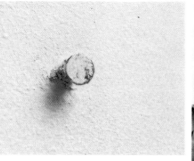

Above: a common problem on gypsumboard walls is that the nails holding the board to the studs pop out. This happens most often as the gypsumboard and stud timber begin to dry and settle.

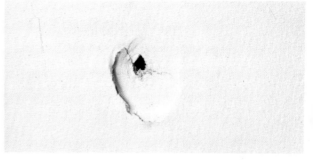

Left: to repair nail pops, first drive nail flush to wall with nail set.

Above: next, drive the nail slightly below surface, making a "dimple" to hold the new plaster.

Below: fill the dimple with patching plaster or patching compound, and smooth with putty knife.

Bottom: let the patch dry for at least 24 hours, and sand smooth.

7. For a smooth coat, pull a putty knife of at least three inches wide across the patch as flatly as possible. To achieve an almost glossy smoothness, wipe a wet sponge across the patch with one hand just ahead of the putty knife held in the other hand. For a rough surface, scour lightly with a paint brush—either in swirling strokes, or jabbed straight at the wall, depending on the texture you are matching.

8. Seal the patch with shellac, or another sealer, before painting.

For Gypsumboard Only

The method of patching shown in the photos at the top of pages 106 and 107 is simple, but works only with gypsumboard.

1. Cut a piece of wallboard three to four inches larger than the hole in both dimensions. Use it as a template with which to square up the hole, and later use it as the patch itself.

2. Cut a piece of plywood as illustrated. Make a $\frac{1}{2}$-inch hole in its center so that you can hold it in place while screwing it behind the solid wallboard.

3. Insert it as shown, and fix it in place with four screws, one on each side.

4. Butter the back of the wallboard patch with patching plaster or spackle. Press it into place.

5. Tack the edges, and spackle as shown.

Patching Deep Holes

The method of patching shown in the photos on the bottom of pages 106 and 107 will work with either plaster walls or gypsumboard where there is no backing, and is applicable for holes up to four inches in diameter.

You will need patching plaster, and a piece of rust-resistant screen, or preferably a piece of *metal lath* that can be purchased from a builders' supply store or lumberyard. Either should be slightly larger than the hole. You

The same conditions that produce nail pops may also cause the tape that seals the joints between panels to lift. First step in repair is to trim off squarely the top of the tape that is still firmly stuck to the stud.

also need a length of wire, a stick, a pair of pliers, and a putty knife.

To prepare the hole, remove all cracked material and plaster just as thoroughly as you can. Before beginning to apply the patching plaster, wet down the wall adjacent to the hole, or you risk shrinkage in your patching material.

After the patch has been finished according to the instructions in the photos on page 107, allow it to dry thoroughly. Then sand smooth with fine sandpaper. Brush patch with sealer before painting.

Repair and Care of Ceramic Tiles

Though ceramic tiles literally last forever, you may find that minor repairs are necessary. You can replace one, or a number of them, easily. In fact, the hardest job in making such a repair may be to find a matching color if your tiles are other than white. It is a good idea when you are having tiling done to ask the contractor to leave a few extra tiles in case repairs are needed later. This will save you the bother of trying to match tiles.

Replacement of loose or broken tiles has been simplified by the use of ready-mixed tile cements. If you are going to reset a loose tile or two, or replace a few broken ones, buy the smallest available can of cement, and a small can of ready-mixed grout (the white material that is used to fill the spaces between tiles).

Resetting Loose Tiles

Scrape off all the old cement from the back and edges of each tile. Butter the back of the tile with a liberal smear of adhesive, and then

Above: the next step is to pull the loose tape gently upward until you reach a spot where the bond is firm again, and cut the tape off exactly square at that point.

Above: measure precisely for a new piece of tape, and cut it to fit as exactly as possible. Apply a thin bonding layer of patching compound, and lay the new tape on it.

Cover the new tape with more patching compound.

Let stand for about 24 hours, then sand smooth.

press firmly into position on the wall. When the adhesive has set hard, fill the open joints around each tile with ready-mixed grout by rubbing it in with your fingertip. Wipe off the excess grout immediately with a damp sponge or cloth.

Replacing a Broken Tile

Start by using the corner of a stiff putty knife to scrape away as much grout as possible around all four sides of the broken tile. Next,

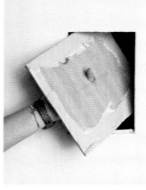
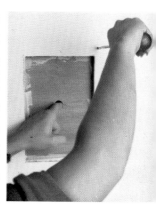

Large holes in gypsumboard require special repair methods, particularly when damage occurs between the wall studs.

Cut a piece of wallboard larger than the hole. Use it as a template to trim hole square; later it will be the patch.

Cut a finger hole in center of piece of $\frac{1}{4}$-inch or $\frac{3}{8}$-inch plywood, and insert it as backing into the hole.

Use finger hole to hold plywood tight against inner surface of wall, and fix it firmly into place with small screws.

tap at the corner of this tile, using a cold chisel and a hammer. In most cases, the corners are not backed up with mortar, so they can be crushed inward without damaging adjacent tiles. Chip away all four corners in this manner until the backing material is exposed. Then remove the center portion by prying up with the chisel, tapping it lightly with the hammer if necessary. After the first piece of tile has been removed, adjacent pieces will come off easily by tapping from the side with the hammer and chisel.

Scrape off as much of the old cement as possible so that the replacement tile with its

backing of adhesive will fit flush with the surrounding tile.

When this has been done, place four fairly generous dabs of new cement on the wall, and press the tile firmly into place. The cement will spread out underneath and form a bonding surface nearly as large as the tile itself.

Let the tile cement set for several hours—overnight if possible—then fill the joints with grout, and wipe away any excess.

When grout must be applied to a larger number of tiles after whole sections have been replaced, it is easier to thin the grouting material slightly with water, and then spread

The first step in an alternate method that is also good for plaster patches is to trim and smooth the hole edges.

Use piece of rustproof wire mesh or metal lath as a packing for patch. Holes in mesh will provide bond for plaster.

Fix wire mesh backing into place with a wooden stick. If the patch is in plaster, moisten the edges of the break.

Lay in the first layer of patching plaster, and work it well into the holes in the mesh so it will make a tight bond.

Left: butter wallboard patch with matching compound on back and edges. Above: fit patch tight against plywood in hole.

Above: tape patch joints, trowel on joint compound or spackle, and feather edges. Let dry at least 24 hours, and then sand.

it over the entire area with an old paintbrush. Rub well into each joint with a soft cloth, then smooth the joints with your fingertip. Wipe off the excess with a damp cloth or sponge until the faces of all the tiles are clean.

Tile Joints

Sinks, shower stall floors, and bathtubs are other sources of trouble. Because of slight settling, or aggressive scrubbing, the grout in these areas sometimes loosens, and falls out. It may also become so dirt-caked that it must be replaced. You can make a neat, watertight job of resealing these joints with silicone rubber caulking materials, available in tubes with a special applicator tip that lets you squeeze out the caulking like toothpaste.

The most endearing trait of ceramic tiles is that they are probably the easiest to clean of all household surfaces. Simply wash them with detergent (soap leaves a film), and warm water. Rinse with clear water, then wipe with an old turkish towel. You can use scouring powder to clean the grouted joints. An old toothbrush is ideal for this. Tile floors should be given a thorough cleaning with household scouring powder at least twice a year, in fact.

Left: when patch has set but is still moist, trim off wires of the mesh. Below: build patch up until it's even with wall.

Below: let dry at least 24 hours (more if you used a lot of compound). Finally, sand smooth and paint to match wall.

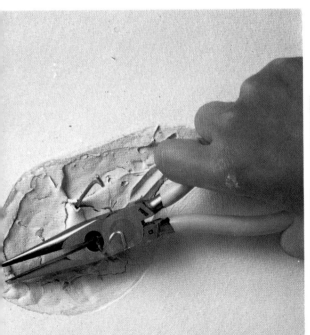

Left: replacement of a cracked wall tile is not too hard to do yourself.

Right: use a punch or a chisel to enlarge hole so that you can lift out the broken tile pieces.

Far right: use the claws of a hammer or a screwdriver to lift out the broken pieces of tile.

While floor tiles are practically impervious to household stains, spills should be wiped up promptly, since there is always the possibility of their penetrating the joints between the tiles. Rust stains on floors and bathroom fixtures can be removed with oxalic acid crystals, which most paint supply stores carry. Make a thin paste by dissolving the crystals in hot water, apply to the stain, and let stand for 15 to 20 minutes. Wipe off and rinse with clear water; repeat this treatment if necessary.

While we are on the subject of tiles, we will also deal with resilient floor tiles, such as vinyl, linoleum, asphalt, and cork. Sooner or later it may become necessary to replace a worn or damaged tile or two of one of these kinds of tiling.

Repairing Resilient Tiles

1. Finding a replacement floor tile of vinyl, linoleum, asphalt, or cork to match the rest is not always easy. If you are really stuck with a floor pattern, style, or color that is not available, a possible solution would be to remove several good tiles, and put in new ones that will make a decorative pattern in the damaged area.

2. Tiles are laid tightly against each other, and the removal of one, if not done carefully, can cause damage to others. To make the job easier, the cement and the tile can first be softened by heat. You can do the job effectively with your electric iron. Set it at high heat, and run it over the tile surface. The object is to loosen the cement, not to melt the tile, so take care this doesn't happen. It is wise to put a damp cloth between the iron and the tile.

3. While the tile is still hot, work the tip of a putty knife under a corner, and carefully pry the tile loose. If it does not come easily—or if you are unable to use heat because of the tile's composition—you may have to cut out the tile in pieces with a hammer and chisel, taking care not to gouge the floor. Begin this operation by first cutting into the seam around the tile with a sharp knife. As you remove the tile with the chisel, work from the center out to the edges. This minimizes the possibility of damage to nearby tiles.

4. Sometimes, if the damaged tile is removed in one piece by the heating method, the cement will be tacky enough so that you can simply press a new tile in its place. Otherwise, scrape off the old cement to provide a smooth base, then put new cement down. Apply it evenly and sparingly to avoid its squeezing up around the edges of the tile, which can make a mess.

5. On linoleum and sheet vinyl, a seam may lift because the cement was not applied properly, or has been weakened by water. You can correct this by applying fresh cement to the area beneath the flooring material, and placing a heavy object on top until it dries. Work the cement in with a flexible blade, taking care not to tear the material. Wipe off the excess, and allow plenty of time to dry. If there is a bubble or raised spot remote from a seam, slit the raised portion along its length with a razor or sharp knife, work the cement under the lifted areas, and press the cut edges back into place.

Wooden Floors

Wood, both hard and soft, is the most widely

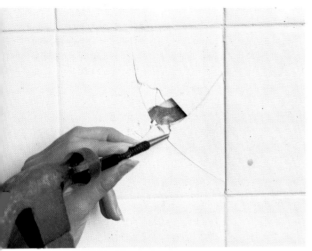

Below: scrape out as much of old cement as you can (not shown), at least enough so new tile and its cement will fit flush. Put four or five generous pats of new cement on the wall backing.

Below: slip replacement tile carefully into position, and press down firmly to spread the cement underneath over entire surface of the tile. Let dry for several hours before applying the grout.

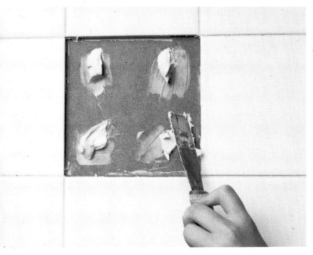

Below: using your fingers and a putty knife, work grout well into the joints around the replacement tile. Scrape off excess. Grout is available in a ready mixed form, but you can also mix your own.

Below: clean any remaining bits of grout off with a damp sponge or rag. The repair should be invisible unless the other tiles are dulled with a layer of grime. That can be cured with a hard scrubbing.

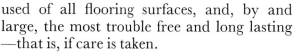

Left: the first problem in replacing a resilient floor or wall tile is to remove it without damaging the tiles around it.

Right: cement holding resilient floor tiles to underlayment can be softened with heat to make removal easier. When using your iron for this purpose, be careful not to melt the tiles. If you do, you will get the bottom of the iron dirty.

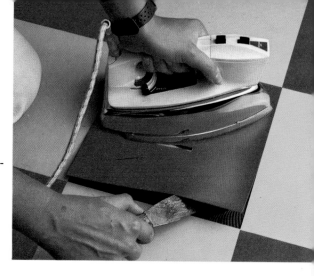

used of all flooring surfaces, and, by and large, the most trouble free and long lasting —that is, if care is taken.

Even with the best of care, however, wood floors eventually become so worn and dirty that they must be sanded down and completely refinished in order to restore their original beauty.

This is a job that is well within the capabilities of the average fixit devotee, provided that she is willing to undertake a fairly ardous job calling for considerable care, and that the necessary machines can be rented. Two machines will be needed: a drum-type floor sander, and a smaller, disc-type edge sander. You can also rent a heavy-duty rotary floor polisher to speed the final waxing job that you will need to do after the final finish has been applied.

Prepare the room by first removing as much as you can from it. The sanding operation will leave a fine film of dust over everything, so, if possible, remove all the furniture. Don't forget to take away pictures, draperies, scatter rugs, and venetian blinds or shades.

Examine the floorboards carefully for protruding nailheads, and countersink any you discover with a fine nail set to avoid tearing the abrasive paper on the sander. Loose, squeaky boards should be tightened by driving three-inch finishing nails into the joint between the boards at a 45-degree angle.

Before you begin the sanding operation, open the windows, and close all doors to the room. This will keep wood dust out of other rooms. Follow the dealer's instructions on how to load the drum with the sandpaper belts. In fact, you should have him show you how to do it, and, if possible, load the drum once under his supervision. At least three different grades of sandpaper will be used. The first serves principally to remove all of the old finish, and is usually a coarse open-coat paper. The other two will be progressively finer grits, which are used to achieve a smooth finish with a second and third sanding. The dealer will supply you with belts of the proper grits. They are quite expensive, but most reputable dealers will take back those you don't use, and give a full refund.

With one possible exception, all sanding should be done with the grain—that is, lengthwise, or parallel, to the floorboards. The exception is for refurbishing an unusually rough or uneven floor. In this case, you should first run the sander at an 45-degree angle to the grain to knock off the worst of the high spots.

Begin sanding along one side of the room. Start near a corner, and work forward and backward from wall to wall. You must start the sander only when the drum is tilted back so that the paper is not in contact with the floor. If you do not observe this rule, the sander will grind a groove into the floor before you get it in motion. When the drum is spinning at speed, move forward slowly, while lowering the drum till it touches the floor. Advance at a steady, even pace till the

Left: after tile has been lifted out, remove as much of old cement as possible. Use a solvent and a putty knife or other kind of scraper.

Above: try the replacement tile in place to make sure it fits right.

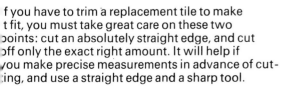

f you have to trim a replacement tile to make t fit, you must take great care on these two points: cut an absolutely straight edge, and cut off only the exact right amount. It will help if you make precise measurements in advance of cutting, and use a straight edge and a sharp tool.

Before applying new cement, warm it to room temperature—70 degrees or more—by letting the can stand in a warm place for several hours. Spread the cement thinly on the underlayment of the floor with a toothed trowel. If you get some cement on the adjacent tiles, clean them well with solvent.

Drop the new tile into position squarely. Be careful not to slide the tile in, or you will push cement up over the edge at some point, and this will smear its surface.

When tile is in place, press the corners down firmly, then press middle. Clean cement smudges at once, then weight the tile and let stand for a few hours.

machine is within a few inches of the baseboard, then raise the drum gradually from the floor before coming to a halt. Now start walking slowly backward while easing the drum down again till it contacts the floor. Pull the machine back along the full length of this first "cut" before moving over to the next stretch. Continue this steady, forward-and-back motion until the entire floor has been roughsanded. I repeat an important caution: *never allow the machine to stop moving while the drum is in contact with the floor. Always start the machine while it is tilted back, so that the drum is off the floor, and wait until the drum is raised off the floor again before bringing the machine to a halt.* Be sure to empty the bag when it is about one-third full.

The large drum sander will do most of the floor, but it will not reach to within the last three or four inches next to the baseboards. It is for this purpose that you need the smaller edging machine. Load it with the same coarse-grit paper as just used on the drum sander, and sand off the small border that is left. Move the machine in a series of brisk semicircular strokes right against the

edge of the quarter-round molding. This will still leave small, unsanded areas in corners and behind radiator pipes, so a hand scraper will be needed for this job.

After the entire floor has been rough sanded, a second smoothing cut is made with a medium-grit paper. Observe the rules about starting and stopping, and, as in the first cut, sand with the grain. Complete all edges with the disk sander, using the same grit paper. Now you are ready for the third and final cut, which is done with finishing grade paper on both the drum sander and the edger.

Before you start to apply the finish to your newly sanded floor, the entire room should be cleaned of all dust with a vacuum cleaner. Don't forget the baseboards, the tops of all door and window frames, and all other woodwork. Dust left in these areas is sure to settle on the wet finish.

Many different types of floor finishing materials are available. Generally speaking they fall into two categories: the penetrating floor sealers, which do not leave a surface film, but soak down into the pores of the

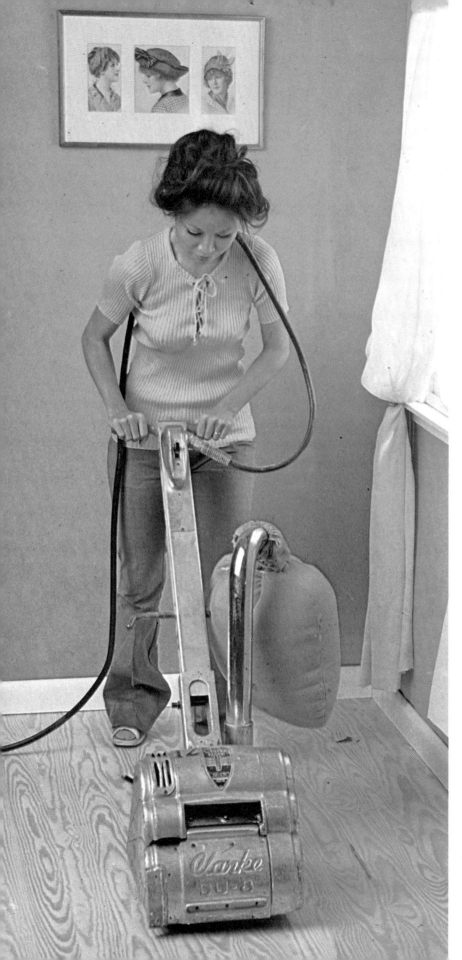

Left: the toughest home repair job is refinishing wooden floors. Yet, even this can be done.

Below: the first step is to drive all protruding nails below surface of floor so that they won't damage either the sander or the sandpaper belts.

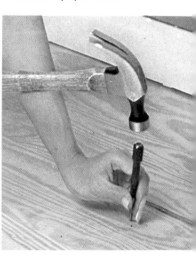

113

You will have to change sandpaper belts several times while sanding, so you must know how to do this. It's a good idea to practice once or twice under supervision of the dealer you rent from.

To change sandpaper belts on the machine from coarse to medium to fine, as necessary, you will need a special wrench to get the belt off the drum. Be sure this wrench is among the equipment.

wood; and the surface finishes, such as varnish, shellac, and certain specialized synthetic finishes. The choice depends on the type of finish preferred for your particular floor, and is best decided after consultation with your dealer.

Whatever the finishing material selected, apply it carefully according to the manufacturer's directions. Allow sufficient drying time, then spread on a thin coat of good quality paste wax. Buff this to a lustrous sheen with a rotary electric polishing machine, which you can also rent.

Taking the Squeak out of Floors

Wood floors that squeak or sag are not only a nuisance, but they can also be dangerous. In many cases you can cure these irritating conditions with a few simple repairs, pro-

vided that you can accurately diagnose the cause of the trouble.

Most floors other than basement floors or concrete floors at ground level actually consist of a double layer of flooring. On top are strips of oak, or other finished hardwood, laid over a rough subfloor of wider boards. The finished flooring fits together with tongue-and-groove joints, held down with nails driven in at an angle along the tongue edge. The nailheads are covered up by the grooved edge of the adjoining board.

The subflooring is nailed diagonally across the tops of the joists, the heavy beams that support the floor. Between the two layers of flooring there is a layer of building paper to keep out dusts and drafts.

If there is a squeaky floor in your house, the problem is usually caused by loose

Above: you will use the disk sander to get at the edges that the big drum sander can't reach. Below: the disk sander uses the same succession of sandpaper grits as does the big drum sander.

Left: after the sanding, floors must be finished. This one was stained, and then sealed to keep the stain from bleeding.

Below: the final coat of varnish being applied.

Right: after you have allowed sufficient drying time for the varnish, all you need is a coat or two of well-buffed wax. Then, once again, you can enjoy beautiful floors that are well-protected.

boards. The trouble may be because the flooring has not been nailed down properly, the subflooring has worked loose so that boards have pulled up from the joists, or a combination of these two in which both finished flooring and subflooring have worked loose.

To silence the squeak temporarily, a dry stainless powdered lubricant can be squirted into the cracks between the offending boards. However, for a more permanent cure, you will have to tighten up the loose boards so that no further movement is possible. The easiest way to do this job is to work from below, provided that the squeaking floor is over an unfinished basement so that joists and floor boards are exposed underneath.

After locating the offending boards by having someone walk around on the floor

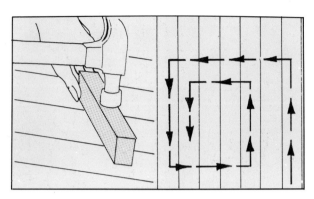

One remedy for squeaking floors starts with locating joists. Place a 2 x 4 block on several thicknesses of paper, and hammer it while moving it around as shown. Sound over joist will be solid.

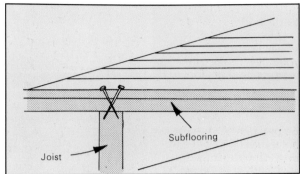

When joists are located, drive 10d finishing nails into them at angles to each other, as though forming a V. Then countersink the nail heads, fill the holes so made with wood putty, and sand.

above while you listen from below, drive thin wooden wedges into the space between the bottom of the floorboard, and the top edge of the joist that supports it. This will tighten the loose boards by taking up slack.

Another way to support floorboards that have bulged upward is to nail a supporting block to the side of the joist. This block should consist of a short length of one-by-three or two-by-four forced tight against the bottoms of the floorboards.

When the loose boards occur at some point between the joists, the cure requires a bridge or crosspiece of two-by-six between the joists, and at right angles to them. Before you nail a bridge of this type in place, drive it upward as high as possible so that its upper edge is tight against the offending floorboards. If necessary, thin wooden wedges can also be driven in place above it to support floorboards that still bulge upward in the center.

If there are loose floorboards on a second story floor, or a first floor that has a finished basement ceiling below, you will have to make the repair from above. After locating the loose boards, drive two 3-inch finishing nails in at an angle so that they form a V. To avoid making unsightly dents in the floor with the hammer head, drive the nails almost all the way in, then finish by driving the heads below the surface with your nail set. It is a good idea to drill pilot holes slightly smaller than the nails to simplify hammering,

and also to help avoid splitting the boards.

Best results are obtained if you can drive the nails into a floor joist, rather than into the subflooring. Locate the joists by tapping the surface of the floor with a block of wood and a hammer. There will be a dull, hollow sound when tapping between the joists. When you are tapping directly over a joist, the sound will be more solid. The joists usually run at right angles to the floorboards, and they are almost always spaced at 16-inch intervals. Holes that remain after the nails have been countersunk should be filled with matching color wood plastic or wood putty to make the job professional looking.

When a floorboard is badly worn or split, the only sure cure lies in cutting out the damaged board, and replacing it with a new piece. This is a job for a carpenter, but a determined handywoman can do it, providing she has the right tools. Drill holes (at least $\frac{1}{2}$ inch in diameter) through the defective board at each end of the damaged section. Drill carefully or you will go through to the subflooring below. Then, using a chisel, carefully split out the defective board without damaging the tongue or groove edge of the boards at either side.

Cut a new length of flooring that will make a snug fit. Trim off the bottom half of the grooved side with a chisel or plane. Now the new piece can be dropped neatly in place from above, and nailed down securely with finishing nails.

Right: the job will be easier, and you will do it neater, if you drill small pilot holes before you drive the nails into joists through floor.

Below: to make the pilot holes, use a fine drill bit having a diameter smaller than a 10d nail.

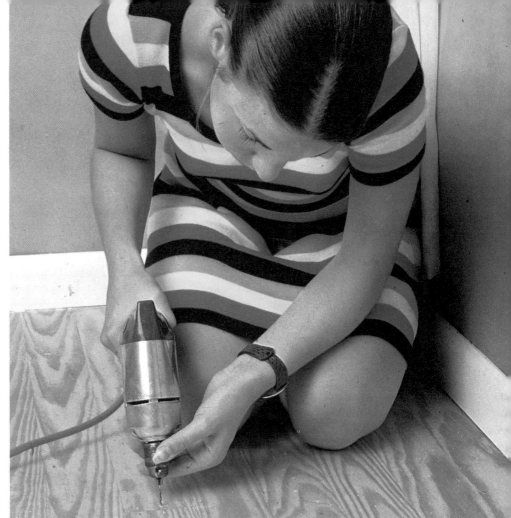

Above: drive nails at an angle, leave nail heads protruding, and sink them with nail set.

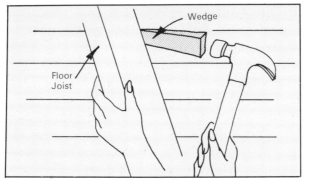

Floor Joist

Wedge

Left: if your floor joists are exposed and accessible, it is easiest to stop squeaks by driving a wooden wedge between joists and subfloor.

Exert strong upward pressure

Supporting Cleat

Joist

Subflooring

Left: if loose boards cause a squeak, butt a 2 x 4 of suitable length against them from below.

How to Keep Your Car Going

9

If you have ever been in this frustrating position, you probably felt like kicking yourself for not paying attention to your car's warning rattles, knocks, and sighs. It's common sense that paying heed to the simple rules of maintenance of your car will save time, money, and temper.

The idea that the care and maintenance of the family car is a job for men only is strictly out of date. Surveys of drivers coming into service stations show that it's women who usually tend to the car's needs—gas in the tank, oil change and lubrication, air in the tires, a tune-up, and other big jobs as they are needed. Surveys also show that—driver for driver—women drive more skillfully and safely than men. Yet we women still seem to know too little about handling car problems and emergencies.

Getting Off to a Good Start

Improper starting procedures can cause problems to develop in your car. Here is a method that will almost always get you off to a good start any time your car has been standing for an hour or more—the so-called cold start.

Before you turn on the ignition and flip the key to start, press the gas pedal all the way to the floor, release it, and engage the start. The engine should kick right off if your car is in good tune. If it doesn't start at once, turn off the ignition, and repeat.

If the car still does not start after a few tries, you may detect an odor of gasoline. This means you probably have flooded the engine. Turn the ignition off, and wait for two or three minutes. Now press the gas pedal all the way to the floor, and hold it there while you engage the starter; don't pump. One or two tries will almost always get results.

Winter starts. When temperatures drop below freezing, starting may be a problem. If your car has been serviced for winter, and the battery is fully charged, try the routine cold

119

When jump starting a car, the correct placement of the battery cables is important. The red cables go to positive poles, the black to negative.

start procedure with two or three prestarting pumps on the accelerator.

If four or five attempts don't get results, don't keep grinding away, because you might run the battery down to the point where it won't start the car at all. Instead, call for service.

Rainy weather starts. After a long rainy spell, moisture may condense on the wires under the hood, causing the spark from the battery to short circuit before it reaches the spark plugs. Lift the hood, and wipe the spark plugs and wires with a dry cloth. If this doesn't bring results, look along the sides of the engine for a black cylinder from which wires lead to the spark plugs. This is the distributor, which delivers power to the

spark plugs in sequence. Under the udderlike cap are two clips that you can spring with a screwdriver. Lift the cap, and dry all exposed parts with a cloth. Now your car should start.

Battery is dead, no start. Before your driving days are over there will come a morning when you turn the starter key and there's only a slow, tired cranking of the engine—or, even worse, no results at all. Your battery is dead, and needs recharging.

In an emergency like this, you can start the car with a procedure known as "jumping the battery". What you need are a set of jumper cables (about $5), and another car that has a live battery. Then follow these steps for starting the car:

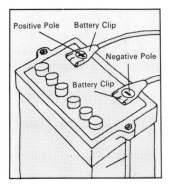

Right: the battery is the heart of the car's electrical system. Keep it filled with distilled water to proper level, and check its cables occasionally to make sure that they are on tight.

Positive Pole — Battery Clip — Negative Pole — Battery Clip

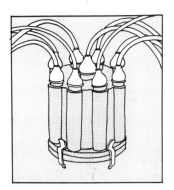

Right: the distributor delivers sparks to each cylinder in turn. Distributor points need periodic renewing by a reliable service agent. Below: use a patented spray can to give the distributor and its various leads an insulation coating. This will give you an easy start even on the dampest of days.

The best position for cars to be in for a jump start is nose to nose. However, if the cables are long enough, the cars can be placed side by side.

1. The two cars must be positioned so that the distance between the batteries can be bridged by the cables. Nose to nose is best.

2. Attach the red cable to the two positive battery posts (marked +), and the black cable to the negative (—) posts.

3. The driver of the car with the good battery starts up and races the motor, while the other driver follows the cold engine starting procedure, repeating if necessary.

4. When the disabled car starts, it should be kept running by racing the engine a little, while the other driver disconnects the cables.

Keep in mind that your battery has not been recharged. Drive to a nearby station immediately, and have the battery checked and recharged.

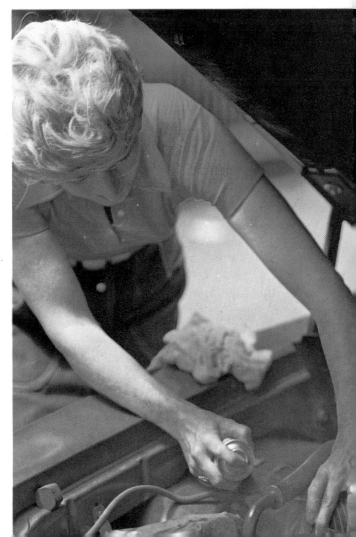

Above: assemble the jack, and pl[...] it under the jacking point. Begin t[...] lift car slowly, with even moveme[...]

Above: changing a flat tire? First thing you should do is to block the wheels at the end opposite to the flat.

Above right: before jacking up the car, remove wheel cover and loosen all the lug nuts; don't take them off.

Changing a Flat

If your driving is limited to short runs around town, chances are that you can get help easily if one of your tires goes flat. Nevertheless, whether you ever have to change a tire or not, you should know how to do it. You must always keep an inflated spare in your car, along with a jack and a lug wrench to remove the flat tire. Even if you don't change the tire, whoever does it will need these tools. Here's how you go about it.

1. Pull well off the road. Passengers except small children, who are safer inside, should get out and stand on the off-road side of the car. If you have a warning device or flare, set it up about 100 feet behind the car.

2. Get out the spare, jack, and lug wrench. Locate two stones or pieces of wood to block the wheels, and place at the end opposite the flat.

3. Pry off the hubcap or wheel cover with the flat end of the lug wrench. Fit the lug wrench firmly over one of the wheel nuts. On

Left: jack up car until flat wheel clears the ground by several inches.

Above: remove lug nuts, and place them in wheel cover for safe keeping.

Right: notice tapered end of lug nut. It goes on toward the wheel.

Right: lug nuts should be tightened alternately. Diagram suggests one sequence. When you have tightened them well, give them an extra turn just for good measure. Above: replace the hub cap, and the job's done. Now remember to get the punctured tire repaired as soon as is possible.

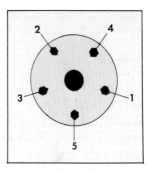

American cars they must be turned counterclockwise to be removed; on foreign cars, turn clockwise. If you can't budge them, try standing on the extension arm of the wrench. If this doesn't work, gently tap each nut with the head of the lug wrench; then turn. Loosen all the nuts with two or three turns, but do not remove them.

4. Assemble the jack, and fit it under the jacking point. Raise the car until the flat tire clears the ground by several inches. If the jack begins to sway or angle off to one side, lower the car, reposition the jack, and raise the car again. Then give the car a gentle push to make sure that it is firmly on the jack.

5. Remove the wheel nuts, and drop them into the wheel cover. Pull the wheel off, and roll it behind the car.

6. Line up the spare wheel so that the holes are in the same position as the studs on the wheel hub. Lift the wheel onto the studs. Replace the nuts so that they are all fingertight, and turn each with the lug wrench.

Lower the car until the spare rests on the ground, but is not carrying the full weight of the car. Tighten the lug nuts. Then, lower the car completely, and give each nut another turn or two with as much force as possible.

Maintaining Your Car

While you may think of your car as a single machine, it is really a system of machines, all of which must work well and in coordination. If your car is to perform reliably and safely, each of the component systems must be serviced and maintained. On pages 124 and

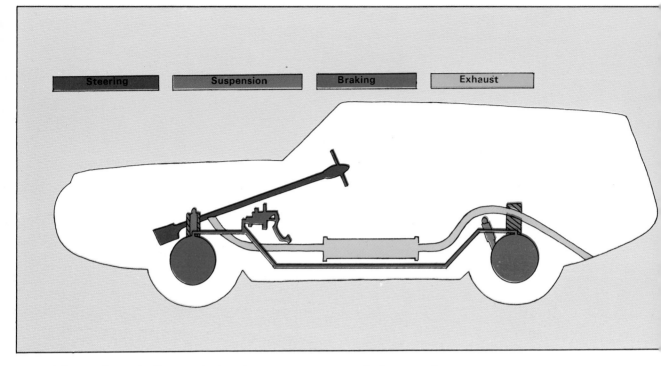

| Steering | Suspension | Braking | Exhaust |

These schematic diagrams isolate the various systems that make up your car, which is a machine containing machines. The systems in this picture are for guidance, control, and extraction of fumes.

125, the diagrams show how your car looks to the eyes of the mechanic who services it.

Using the color key as a guide, follow each system through its related parts. As each system is outlined and described, you will understand better what you, the driver, must do to keep it functioning well.

1. *Ignition or Electrical System.* This makes the engine start, and runs all the electrical items in and on your car. Power flows from the battery, which gets renewed strength, in turn, by way of the alternator (or generator).

Your responsibility is to report any sign of trouble, to detect tired action from the battery, and to arrange for a tune-up at least once a year, including the spark plugs, distributor, and ignition timing.

2. *Cooling System,* A car engine creates heat. To cool it, water bathes the hot (or moving) parts. This water is cooled by air that is pulled in through the radiator by the fan, turned by a belt operated by the engine. You must see that the outside of the radiator is kept clean, and you must replace a worn fan

belt or radiator cap, have water added to the radiator when it's needed, and follow the instruction manual concerning antifreeze.

3. *Fuel System.* Gasoline flows through the fuel line, and is forced by the fuel pump into the carburetor. Here it is turned into vapor, and then ignited by the electrical system to produce power.

Your responsibility is to have this system checked to keep it in efficient working order. If you are troubled by frequent stalling, the carburetor may need adjusting.

4. *Power System.* When the gas-and-air mixture is fired, it forces down the pistons and rods, which rotate the crankshaft.

Your responsibility is to have your engine serviced on schedule, and to make sure that the oil is changed at recommended intervals. Have the crankcase flushed once a year, and, most important of all, maintain the oil level between changes. Any unusual oil consumption calls for immediate attention.

5. *Drive System.* The "drive train" consists of the transmission, drive shaft, the universal joint connecting these two, and the differential that permits the back wheels to turn at different speeds when you turn corners. The purpose of the system is to convert the power

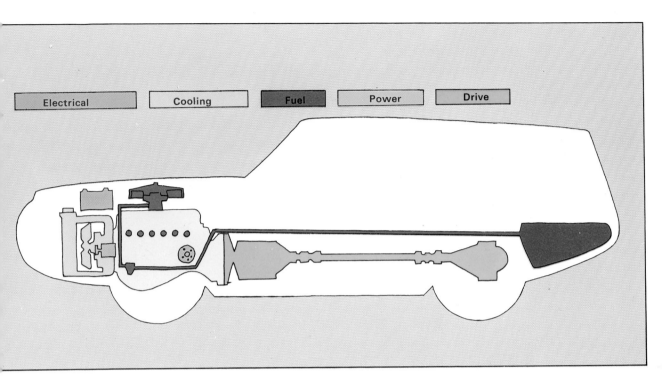

| Electrical | Cooling | Fuel | Power | Drive |

produced in the power system into motion.

Your responsibility is to have the drive system inspected when your car is serviced, and to have maintenance done as needed. The level of transmission fluid should be checked from time to time. Rough shifting, slipping of gears, or grinding must be reported to your car mechanic immediately.

6. *Steering System.* Besides the steering wheel, the guidance system of your car consists of the steering post and its gears, which are designed so that a small person can turn a large car with little effort. The front wheels and tires also belong to the steering system.

Your responsibility is to take your car in for inspection and service when you notice any unusual play in the steering wheel, or any tendency of the car to pull right or left, which indicates the wheels are out of balance. Even without such warnings, wheel alignment should be checked every six months. Tires must be kept inflated at the pressure recommended in the owner's manual, and also should be rotated regularly.

7. *Suspension System.* The shock absorbers and springs are essential to a smooth ride, and to proper steering. They function to smooth out the effects of bumps and rough roads by

Your car will run smoothly and safely when all its systems are functioning properly, which is assured by maintenance. The systems shown in this picture are for starting up and keeping the car in motion.

absorbing and damping the vibrations.

Your responsibility is to take note of any unusual pitch and sway when you turn a corner, or a ride that's unduly bouncy. These, as well as an obvious sag to one side, may indicate that your car has a broken "shock" absorber or spring. Prompt attention is necessary.

8. *Braking System.* When your foot goes on the brake, it stops the front and back wheels through a hydraulic device. "Hydraulic" means something that uses fluid to operate; in a car the liquid is called "brake fluid." Also in the braking system are the parts that stop the wheels. This is where brakelining is used; it is a material that may wear out, and have to be replaced.

Your responsibility is to watch your brake action, and report to your service station if it is slow, "spongy," or if your foot goes closer than two inches to the floor when you put on the brake. When your car is given a complete checkup, usually twice a year, the braking system should be included.

9. *Exhaust System.* This is the system that draws off burned gases and residues from the engine, and sends them out the rear end of your car. It's made up of the exhaust manifold, the exhaust pipe, the muffler, and the tailpipe.

Your responsibility is to have the system checked for breaks or cracks, which could leak deadly carbon monoxide into the car. Proper maintenance of this system can help cut down on air pollution.

Some Tips on Driving

Before passing another car on the road, be sure your way is clear for a long way ahead. Use directional signals when passing, and take a last-minute glance in your outside mirror before changing lanes. Move back into the right lane only when you can see all of the car you've passed in your rear view mirror. Don't forget to switch off your signals so they won't continue to blink.

Allow for high speeds by everyone, and in every move you make. When entering a fast road, build up speed before merging into onmoving traffic. When space permits, blend smoothly into the right lane, picking up the pace.

Around Town. Most accidents happen within 10 minutes of home. In traffic, know what's going on around you. Be in the correct lane well before making a turn. Don't let down your caution because you're on a familiar street. Never crowd—or, as it is commonly called, tailgate—the car ahead. If someone does this to you, slow up and let him by. Think ahead. Know where you yourself are going, and anticipate at all times what others may do.

Winter. Drive with care. Adjust your speed to the conditions. Carry something heavy, such as a bag of sand, to give traction if you get stuck. Use snow tires or the newer studded type. In a skid, keep your foot off the brake or, at the most, move it lightly up and down. To straighten your car out, turn your front wheels to the right if the back of the car is sliding to the right, or left, if that's the way it's swerving.

Start off slowly to get the feel of the road. Take corners gently. Never go down hard on your brake.

Begin the winter with a strong battery, and keep it charged. In most parts of the country, antifreeze must go in your radiator. Your service station can tell you how much antifreeze to use, and when.

Night, Fog, Rain. You should always keep your windshield wipers and washers in good working condition. This includes a change of wiper blades from time to time. In less-than-perfect weather, adjust your speed to conditions—especially to visibility. Put your lights on full so others can see you. If lights

Accidents will happen (far left), but you can minimize your chance of being in one—as well as increase your driving pleasure—by following a few simple rules for safe and sane driving. Among them are: test your brakes after going through deep puddles (left); don't tailgate (right); have your car winterized in autumn to prepare for snow (below). Make sure, too, that your headlights and dimmer switches work. Also keep windshield clean, and the wiper blades in good working condition.

coming at you are dazzling at night, look at the right-hand edge of the road, rather than straight ahead. This helps in fog as well, since the road level may be clear of fog.

Ten Safe Driving Tips

The following 10 points are especially important for all drivers to keep in mind.

1. Be courteous. Accidents would be cut in half if all drivers practiced good manners.

2. Always use your safety belt.

3. If a tire blows out, hold firmly to the wheel to prevent swerving into traffic. Let the car slow down naturally, with your foot off the brake, and then ease off the road.

4. Insist that children behave while in a moving car, and don't let them interfere with the driver in any way.

5. Always put your parking brake on firmly; if you are out of the car and it begins to roll, don't try to stop it.

6. Carbon monoxide is deadly, so never run your car in a closed garage, and always open a window a crack when driving.

7. Put your full headlights on at dusk, in rain, and in fog so other drivers can see you.

8. Keep space around your car at all times. Never tailgate.

9. Avoid driving when sleepy, tense, or upset.

10. When driving alone, know your route, stop for breaks, and don't try to cover excessive distances.

Questions & Answers

Have you ever sat in a cold house during a power failure, feeling helpless about the fact that the water pipes were probably freezing? Would you know what to do if your roof started to leak just above your expensive rug while a storm raged? Are you aware of the action to take for everyone's safety if you smell a gas leak?

When emergency situations occur in the home, you should be prepared to administer "household first aid" until such time as you can permanently repair a fault, or have it corrected by a professional. Quick action on your part can prevent costly damage to materials, furnishings, equipment, and health. It is the purpose of this first part of *The Fixit Book's* final section to arm you with the first aid measures you need to know to keep things going until further help comes.

There's another kind of emergency that might confront any family without warning, and that is a natural disaster: a flood, earthquake, or hurricane, for example. While no one should worry unduly about possible calamities, such events do occur. If you are caught in one, there are ways that you can better meet the crisis, and, perhaps, prevent a tragic loss.

The second part of this section, then, gives you advice and guidance on how to behave for greatest safety in the face of nature gone wild. The recommendations have been gathered from the American Red Cross, the National Safety Council, the U.S. Public Health Service, and the U.S. Army Corps of Engineers.

Of course, the section would be incomplete without some practical tips and hints on taking care of things around the home in the ordinary course of daily life, both to keep them from going wrong, and to repair them yourself when they do. As we all know, proper maintenance and proper use prevents many a bad situation from developing. So, you will find valuable information on many maintenance questions. More, you will find answers to problems on gutters and downspouts, insect control, small electric appliances, window screens, and other troubles.

Part of the fixit scene is regular maintenance of your home, of which the handywoman can do much. Such care can often avert serious repairs.

129

Emergencies and Natural Disasters

Last winter our heating system broke down, and our water pipes froze. How can I guard against this in future heating or power breakdowns?

If the heating system should break down, or a power blackout occur, water pipes must be protected from freezing. Opening the taps a bit will help, since flowing water is less likely to freeze. In a pinch, pipes in the coldest parts of the house—the basement or an un-insulated crawl space—can be wrapped loosely with several sheets of newspaper over-lapped and tied at the ends as insulation.

If the electrical power or heating system is off for a prolonged period of time in sub-freezing weather, the plumbing system should be completely drained. A drain valve is usually provided at the low point of the supply piping for this purpose. Pumps, storage tanks, hot water tanks, toilet tanks, hot water and steam heating systems, and other water system appliances or accessories, should also be drained. Put antifreeze in all fixture and drain traps.

Once frozen, how can pipes be thawed most safely?

The best method of thawing water that has frozen inside pipes is to apply an electric heating cable to the pipes. Wrap the cable around so that the entire length of the pipe can be thawed at one time. Leave the cable in place to supply continuous heat during extremely cold weather.

A propane torch can also be used, but exercise extreme caution. Never concentrate the torch's heat on a single section of pipe; the water within may become hot enough to generate steam under pressure, and rupture the pipe. Keep the torch moving, and at a safe distance from the pipe. Also be careful that the flame does not scorch or set fire to surrounding wood framing.

A safer method of thawing frozen pipes is to cover them with rags, and then pour hot water over the rags. Whatever method you use, first open a faucet beyond the frozen point, and begin the thawing operation there. The open faucet will permit steam to escape, thus reducing the chance of the buildup of dangerous pressure. Do not allow the steam to condense and refreeze before it reaches the faucet.

I know a gas leak is serious, so what should be done if you smell gas?

Get everybody out of the house—the stronger the smell, the greater the urgency. If possible, turn the thermostat way down so that the furnace does not come on, because it could set off an explosion if it does. Call the gas company, immediately, from a neighbor's phone if possible. If this is not practical, and the gas smell is not too strong, hold a handkerchief over your nose, go back into the house, dial the operator to report the trouble, and get back outside immediately. Do not go back into the house again until the gas company has repaired the leak.

Can you tell me how to repair roof leaks in an emergency situation?

High winds often rip roof shingles loose, allowing water to seep through the roof and into the attic. If you can get onto the roof to make a temporary repair, replace the damaged or missing shingles, and cover the affected area with a plastic or rubber sheet that you slip underneath the shingles above them; staple the ends of the sheet down. Caulk around the edges of the sheet to prevent water from being driven under it.

When ice or snow conditions do not allow you to correct the problem from above, you can locate the leak in an exposed attic or crawl space. Apply waterproof sealer from a can or tube, which should be in your household repair kit, and work it well into and around the area to keep out water at least until the storm abates.

130

I've always dreaded the thought of a fire in my home, and often wonder how I would behave in the emergency. What are some of the things I should try to remember to do?

First, shout "fire!" as loudly as possible. Arouse everyone immediately, and get them outside. *Do not linger to save possessions!*

Call the fire department. In most cases, you simply dial the operator. Give her your address clearly.

If the fire is confined to a small area, and you have a safe and sure exit available, use any available extinguisher to fight the flames until the firemen arrive. But be certain you know what you are doing. For example, it is wrong to use water to try to douse a grease fire—it will only spread the flames. Skip this step completely unless your own safety, and that of your family, is assured.

Some of these suggestions may seem elementary, but they bear endless repeating. Too often a person, in the panic of the moment, will try to extinguish a fire himself. By the time he realizes the futility of this, and calls the fire department, it may be too late. Worse yet, members of the family in other parts of the house may be trapped because they were not warned in time to leave.

The real key to avoiding a disaster is prevention. Make sure that every member of the family knows exactly what to do in a fire emergency. Have an alternate escape route for every room. Rooms on upper floors should have windows that are easily opened. Rope ladders should be placed in all dead-end rooms, and children should be trained in their use.

I am a new resident in an earthquake area, and would like to have some guidance about what to do if an earthquake occurs.

If you are indoors when an earthquake starts, stand beneath a strong doorway, or against inside walls, or get under a heavy piece of furniture such as a desk, table, or bed. Stay away from windows. Do not stand near masonry walls and chimneys. At all times look out for falling objects, such as structural materials and bricks.

If you are outside, move away from buildings, utility wires, and any objects that could topple, such as towers. Stay in the open until the shaking stops. Do not run through or near buildings. The greatest danger from falling debris is just outside doorways, and close to outer walls.

If you are in a moving car, stop in an open area away from buildings, utility poles, and overpasses, and stay in the car.

When the quake is over, check for fires and fire hazards. Examine gas, water, and electricity lines. If they are turned on, shut them off until you are sure everything is safe. Be particularly wary of gas leaks, and do not use any open flame. Do not operate electrical switches until you are sure there is no danger of leakage.

If you smell gas, open windows, and shut off the main valve. Leave the building, and report the leak; do not reenter.

If water pipes are damaged, shut off the main water valve. If electrical wiring is damaged, or if there is a short circuit, shut off the electricity. Do not touch downed power lines, or anything in contact with them.

In low-lying coastal areas there is danger of tidal waves after an earthquake. Start for high ground as soon as the shaking stops.

What should we do to be better prepared for a flood?

If you live in a coastal area or river plain subject to flooding, you should keep in touch with the weather situation during periods of heavy storms. Listen to local radio or TV for flood warnings and instructions. If a flood warning is on, fill your car's fuel tank. Store water in clean bathtubs, cooking utensils, bottles, and jars. Stock a supply of convenience foods requiring no refrigeration. Keep battery-powered portable radio, flashlights, and candles handy. Install check valves in sewer traps.

If told to evacuate, do so immediately, after turning off electricity, gas, and water. If time permits, move furniture, rugs, and valuables to a higher level within the house.

If your area is subject to flash floods, and a warning is issued, leave immediately. If your car stalls, abandon it immediately, and seek higher ground.

If driving, look out for damaged roads, slides, and fallen wires. Do not try to drive through flood water.

If walking, do not try to cross a road or stream where water is over your knees; avoid fallen wires.

After the flood, do not eat food that has been touched by flood water. Boil drinking water. Keep tuned to local radio for instructions. Stay away from disaster areas.

How can we have some preparedness for a hurricane?

During hurricane season, listen to the radio for Weather Service advice; keep your car's fuel tank full; store emergency supplies of food and water; have flashlights, candles, and battery-powered radio handy.

When a hurricane warning is issued, stay tuned to local radio or TV. Board up windows, or cover them with storm shutters. Secure outdoor objects that might blow away. Put car in garage. Evacuate shoreline and low-lying areas that might be affected by waves or tides. Moor your boat and leave it. Store emergency drinking water in clean bathtubs, cooking utensils, jars, and bottles.

During a hurricane stay indoors, away from windows. Open windows opposite the wind side. If your house is not a sturdy structure, go to a designated shelter. Do not stay in a mobile home. Before evacuating, turn off electricity, gas, and water; lock doors.

If the storm dies suddenly, beware: this may only mean that the eye of the hurricane is directly overhead. Stay inside; winds will resume from the opposite direction. Close open windows, and open windows on the opposite side of the house.

After the hurricane, avoid downed electric wires. Be alert for damaged roads and slides. Report damaged electric wires, gas and water pipes, and sewers. Avoid disaster areas. Use phone for emergencies only. Don't drive unless necessary.

The threat of tornadoes is a real one in our area. What is your advice on facing this emergency?

Tornadoes are often preceded by darkened skies, and winds blowing from the south, combined with rain, hail, and lightning. Tornadoes usually strike between noon and midnight. If you live in a tornado belt, stay tuned to local radio and TV stations for tornado alerts.

If a tornado warning is issued, get inside as quickly as possible. Open windows on the side of the house away from the storm's approach. Take refuge in the basement near the wall in the most sheltered and deepest part. Stay under a sturdy table or workbench. If you have no basement or cellar, take cover in the smallest room with stout walls. The first floor is safer than higher floors. Lie under a heavy table, desk, bed, or tipped-over upholstered chair or sofa, against inside walls in center of house. Stay away from windows. Keep tuned to a battery-powered radio for emergency bulletins.

Away from home, take shelter in a steel-frame or reinforced concrete building. In open country, move away from tornado's path at a right angle. If you can't escape, lie flat in a ditch and shield your head; also cover your face with clothing to prevent suffocation from dust. Do not stay in a car, trailer, or mobile home. Stay out of buildings with wide-span roofs, such as theaters and gymnasiums.

Maintenance

How can I keep the kinds of repairs that require professional handling to a minimum?

In most areas of life, it does not pay to look for trouble. Home maintenance, however, is one field in which looking for trouble may bring you benefits, rather than just more trouble. Some parts of a house are more prone to wear and deterioration than other parts, and you should know where they are. More important than knowing, you should inspect these sections regularly—in most cases, at least once a year—to try to detect problems before they become major. Then you can make the determination as to whether you can make repairs yourself, or call in the professional.

Typical of the areas requiring periodic inspection are:

The roof. This should be inspected in the spring and fall, and after any severe storms, for bent or broken shingles, loose flashing, and the like. Roof problems that are ignored can become magnified many times, causing deterioration of sheathing and rafters, and also causing damage to the ceilings and walls inside.

Gutters and downspouts. If these are not properly carrying away roof water, damage may be caused to foundation plantings or gardens. In addition, wood may become rotted in areas where water is allowed to accumulate.

Chimneys and flues. Stopped-up flues can cause heavy smoke damage; keep them clean. Chimneys should last as long as the house, but the mortar between bricks must be re-pointed occasionally. Also check for cracks now and then, especially after there has been a severe storm.

Television antenna. A properly installed antenna should withstand all but the most violent wind and storms. Give it the once-over every year to make sure it's up securely. and that all supports are tightly fastened.

Windows, doors, shutters. Small cracks should be repaired before they become big holes, and loose hinges fixed before the door falls off. Small sections of rotted wood should be scraped clean and patched. These chores should be part of a general spring or fall checkup; if you let them go, you will wind up replacing the whole door, shutter, or what-ever.

Plumbing and drains. Periodic cleanouts are cheaper and easier than having to resort to an electric auger, or calling a plumber, after the drain is completely stopped up.

Septic tanks and cesspools. Do not do much beyond adding chemicals, as recommended, on a regular basis. Have an expert inspect them once a year.

Paint. You can let inside painting go for a good while before serious damage results, although your rooms may look pretty bad. But outside, paint is vital to the preservation of the wood siding and trim, unless it is of redwood and red cedar. Check the exterior paint yearly, and spot-prime any bare areas. Plan on painting the outside every three to five years, preferably in the fall.

The attic. Sometimes a roof will seem perfectly sound from the outside, yet an inspection of the attic will disclose telltale dark splotches on the underside of the sheathing; perhaps it will even be wet after a recent rain. Try to determine where the leak originates. It may not be directly above the wet spot because water often runs along a rafter or other framing member before it becomes visible. If the leak is near a valley where two roofs adjoin, or near a roof opening, such as for a chimney or a plumbing vent, strongly suspect the metal flashing. This can be patched with asphalt compound, but if it shows signs of irreparable old age, it's better to replace it.

If all efforts to find the source of a roof leak fail, you may have to tear off some of the shingles in the suspect area, and inspect underneath. If you still cannot pinpoint the problem, call in a professional roofer. Under no circumstances should you give up, and let the problem go uncorrected.

Basement or crawl space. Check for damp spots or cracks on concrete or masonry foundations and floors that may indicate leakage. Patch cracks so that water will not penetrate and freeze, causing further damage. Check all exposed framing, particularly that which is in contact with masonry, or is close to the ground. Decay usually starts low, and then spreads to the rest of the house.

What are some of the methods that can be used to control annoying and damaging household insect pests?

Because most insect pests are adept at keeping themselves hidden, it is much more difficult to get rid of them after they become established inside the house. For this reason, prevention is by far the wisest—and simplest—method of control. In most cases the preventive program will consist of three parts: eliminating breeding places and points of entry; eliminating sources of food by proper housekeeping techniques; and using the proper insecticide when treatment does become necessary.

The chart on the next page lists some of the more common insect pests, briefly describes their characteristics, and lists control techniques for each. Since good housekeeping and proper sanitation are an important part of any pest control program, thorough cleaning of all corners and crevices where spilled food or organic matter can collect is essential. This will eliminate places that the insects can hide and feed. Particular attention should be paid to corners in cupboards and closets, as well as to openings under baseboards, in floors, and behind kitchen drawers. Another place that needs frequent cleaning is the space under the kitchen and bathroom sinks, and around all water pipes, toilets, and other plumbing fixtures. Special care in these spots will never be wasted.

All food should be stored in tightly closed containers, as should garbage and other waste material. Accumulation of trash or refuse against the outside of the house can provide a ready breeding ground for many insect pests, and may provide a convenient means of entry into the house itself. To close up as many of these entry points as possible, caulking compound should be used to seal up permanently as many openings as possible, especially where pipes or utility lines pass through foundation walls.

Insect pests may also be carried into the house in cartons, or in packages of groceries and other purchases. Cockroaches and silverfish, for example, may be hidden in the seams or crevices of a cardboard carton. From here they will crawl out to establish colonies that will eventually infest the entire home. Moth larvae may be hidden in dirty clothing that is brought back from a summer home or resort. Before storing, these should be thoroughly cleaned or laundered.

When in spite of all preventive measures insects do invade the home, insecticides of various types will be required to control or eliminate them. Generally speaking, these fall into one of two categories: surface sprays, or space sprays.

As its name implies, a surface spray is applied to surfaces inside the home where insects tend to crawl or congregate. The liquid wets the surface, and leaves a deposit that can kill insects coming in contact with it even after a period of weeks has elapsed. Surface sprays may be applied with a hand spray gun, or with a pressurized spray can. Many types can also be applied with an ordinary paint brush, though tests should be made first to make certain that no damage will occur on some types of floor tiles, and on some plastics.

Space sprays are designed for flying insects, such as mosquitoes and houseflies. They form a fine mist that remains suspended in the air for long periods of time so that flying insects will contact them while still in flight. Since they leave little or no residue when dry, they are not suitable for use as a surface spray, and have no lasting effect. Most of the widely sold brands are available in aerosol cans, though a properly designed hand spray gun can be used if extra economy is desired.

When using any spray, always cover all food, cooking and eating utensils, and cooking and eating surfaces. Space sprays should be applied while windows and doors are closed, and they should be used according to the directions on the container. To prevent adverse effects, the homeowner should leave the room immediately after spraying, and the room should be left closed and unoccupied for at least half an hour before anyone reenters.

Insect Control

Insect	Characteristics	Control Methods
Houseflies	Breed in food, garbage, and decaying organic matter; are frequent carriers of human diseases.	Equip garbage cans with tight covers, and do not let food stand uncovered. Keep screens on all openings. Use space or aerosol spray to kill flies indoors.
Mosquitoes	Breed in stagnant water during spring, summer, and fall. Besides biting, some types carry disease.	Pools of water should be eliminated, covered, or sprayed. Gutters should be cleaned to prevent puddles. Aerosol spray can be used indoors.
Ants	Breed in nests indoors or outdoors. Usually follow same path to food supply, so can be traced carrying food back.	Seal cracks and openings through which they can enter. Apply liquid insecticide containing chlordane, lindane, diazanon, dieldrin, or malathion. Apply as surface spray along path, and near openings.
Spiders	Except for black widows, most are harmless to humans in U.S. Black widows are black, about $\frac{1}{2}$-inch long, and have a globular body.	Remove piles of loose trash from yard, and knock down webs when noticed. Use liquid spray containing chlordane, lindane, or dieldrin.
Cockroaches	Vary from $\frac{1}{2}$ to 2 inches in length, and from yellowish brown to black. They hide in dark places, and come out at night to feed on human food, garbage, starch, or glue in cartons.	Periodical cleaning of all corners and crevices to eliminate dirt. Apply surface spray containing diazinon, malathion, or ronnel. A pyrethrum spray in crevices will drive them out into the open.
Clothes Moths and Carpet Beetles	Larvae of both these insects feed on wool, mohair, fur, and a wide range of clothing and furnishings. They vary in color from yellowish to brown, and grow to about $\frac{1}{2}$ inch.	Frequent cleaning of rugs, closets, radiator enclosures, and upholstery. Use stainless protective spray containing DDT, methoxychlor, or Perthane. Store clothing and woolens in airtight chest or closet, and enclose napthalene flakes or balls, or paradichlorobenzene crystals.
Bedbugs	Brown, flat bugs, $\frac{1}{4}$- to $\frac{3}{8}$-inch long. They feed on human blood. Their bites cause itching. Lay eggs in crevices, and around tufts in mattresses.	Apply surface spray containing DDT, lindane, malathion, or pyrethrum. Mattresses should be covered, but not soaked. Spray must not contain more than 0.1 per cent lindane or 1 per cent malathion.
Silverfish	Slender wingless insects less than $\frac{1}{2}$-inch long, and shiny or pearl gray in appearance. Active at night, they like cool places, and eat anything that is high in protein, sugar, or starch. Will frequently eat paper and bookbindings.	Use surface spray containing chlordane, DDT, dieldrin, heptachlor, lindane, or malathion. Spray closets, baseboards, and places where pipes go through walls.

It seems to me that insect control is an important part of house maintenance, especially since a great deal of damage can be caused by termites and fungus. Can you tell me about such house pests and their control?

The structural wooden timbers of your house can be seriously damaged by two natural pests. One is the termite, and the other is a fungus called dry rot. Since the damage they cause is similar, let us treat them together in talking about control.

Both problems are serious, and when they become noticeable, demand drastic and immediate attention. A basic cause of both conditions is excessive moisture. Particularly susceptible are homes located near rotted lumber—perhaps stumps or construction scraps that are buried next to the foundation because of careless backfilling. Wooden steps, or fences in direct contact with the ground, are also invitations to termites, whose staple food is wood.

In addition, if any conditions of dampness are allowed to go unchecked, the danger of termites or dry rot is greatly increased. Unfortunately, this type of problem is often discovered too late. Termites eat wood from within, and, except for kings and queens of their colonies, never surface. Thus damage may go unnoticed until a structural member is practically hollowed out. This process takes some time, however—perhaps years— and vigilance is a good defense.

If you suspect problems of this nature, inspect all wood under the first floor of your home. Probe any suspicious areas with an ice pick, or a sharp knife. If the probe penetrates easily for more than about an inch under hand pressure, the wood has probably deteriorated.

To reach wood not in direct contact with the ground, termites build mud tubes or channels from the ground up along the foundation walls to the house sills. Whenever these are found, they should be broken open. Then check the adjacent wood areas for damage.

During mating season, the kings and queens leave the colonies to establish new ones. These winged insects are often confused with flying ants, but a close inspection will show that the termites are thicker waisted, and have opaque, whitish wings, while the ant's wings are transparent. When they settle down in their new communities, the termites shed their wings. If you find a pile of such tiny wings near your foundation, this is another sure sign of trouble with these wood-eating insects.

Termites thrive on wood, but they cannot live in it, and must return to the soil at least once a day. Therefore, your most effective defense against them is to poison the soil around your house so that they cannot penetrate it. There are several preparations for this. Most effective are those containing chlordane or heptachlor. Whichever you use, carefully follow manufacturer's directions for mixing and diluting. A trench two to three feet deep must be excavated around the entire foundation. Part of the poison is poured into the bottom of the trench, and the remainder is mixed with the soil as it is replaced. This will provide protection for up to five years, and any termites remaining inside the house will quickly die off as they are prevented from returning to their colonies.

Dry rot is caused by a microscopic fungus growth. It is a harmless airborne organism until it finds damp wood. Then it multiplies and grows rapidly, feeding on the cellulose of the moist lumber. Dry rot is almost impossible to detect until it is in the advanced stages. Then the wood will have a spongy, cheeselike consistency when probed with ice pick or knife.

Wood that has been damaged by termites or dry rot must be replaced, after the conditions that have caused the damage are corrected. If the wood that has been damaged is an integral part of the house structure— joists or sills, for example—a professional contractor may have to be employed. You might want to use especially treated lumber to avoid a similar kind of problem in the future.

I read somewhere that it hardly pays to repair small appliances, and that the aim should be to prolong their life by proper care and use. What about this?

Such a viewpoint is correct. In most cases, it's just about as cheap to buy a new toaster or electric coffee maker as it is to have one repaired, particularly if the repair requires two or three hours of work at $4 to $6 an hour. What about making repairs at home? Except for the few appliances that are made especially with replaceable component modules, there is not much that can be done at home beyond making simple repairs to the cord or wall plug. With some appliances, even that is a difficult task. Other problems usually involve switches, automatic controls, timers, and thermostats, which are generally beyond the skills and knowledge of the do-it-yourself enthusiast.

Routine maintenance, however, will give your toaster or coffee maker a longer life, and will go a long way toward preventing untimely breakdowns. Maintenance really means intelligent use—for example, remembering to disconnect appliances by grasping the plug, rather than jerking on the cord. Of course, you should watch long cords to keep them from kinking and twisting, and to make sure they are not being sawed back and forth over rough or sharp surfaces. Care of this kind is particularly important to observe when using your iron or vacuum, for the cords on both of these appliances are subject to unusually hard wear.

Appliances that hold food or beverages at a certain temperature—such as electric coffee makers, food warmers, casseroles, and fryers—should be turned off when not in use. Even better, disconnect them. Pop-up toasters often fail to work because the insides are jam-packed with crumbs from breakfasts long past. Clean your toaster regularly.

Dirt-clogged vacuum cleaners are the greatest cause of poor operation. Empty the bag often, and don't let it get packed solid. A full bag sharply reduces dirt pickup ability, and also strains the motor. If dirt gets into the motor itself, usually as the result of an overloaded bag, the motor will overheat and run down. If the motor labors, or feels excessively hot, it's usually time for the bag to be emptied or replaced.

If your unit uses disposable bags, it's best to use only the manufacturer's replacement bags made especially for your machine. A substitute type may have a poor fit, and allow dirt to get into the motor.

My husband and I are planning to move to a suburban area that doesn't have municipal sewers, and we may have a cesspool or septic tank. What is the difference between these two, and what should we know about the maintenance of whichever one our new home has?

Homes built away from city sewage lines, which includes all rural homes, and a great many suburban ones, must depend on a private sewage system to handle waste disposal from the household plumbing system. One of two types of disposal systems will be installed: a cesspool, or a septic tank. A basic knowledge of how each of these operates, as well as some pointers on their care and maintenance, will help you avoid annoying and expensive breakdowns, and will assure you of a safe and sanitary system.

A *cesspool* consists of a simple covered pit that has its sides lined with masonry blocks laid with mortar. The household sewer line discharges raw sewage directly into this pit. The liquid portion is then disposed of by seeping, or leaching, into the surrounding soil. Solids settle to the bottom, and are retained inside the pit.

Because they allow raw sewage to seep directly into the surrounding soil, cesspools can be used only in porous or sandy soils, never in swampy areas, or in heavy clay soils. They must be located at least 150 feet away from wells, and 15 to 20 feet away from building foundations. Some communities forbid cesspools entirely, while others limit their depth and location. The local Health Department will usually supply complete information on any restrictions that must be observed.

The cesspool begins to fill up and overflow when the openings in its masonry wall clog up with grease, or other insoluble material. Pumping out or emptying the cesspool may give only temporary relief, since such action does not always eliminate the cause of the clogging. As a result, the cesspool often refills rapidly. To eliminate this, an entirely new cesspool may have to be built, or a second one connected to the old one to dispose of the overflow.

Septic tanks provide a more satisfactory method of home sewage disposal. They are designed to decompose solids, and treat sewage by bacterial action, before it seeps away into the earth. The tank itself is usually built of masonry or steel, and it is water-tight in construction. As sewage from the house line enters the tank, solids separate from the liquid, and settle to the bottom. Bacterial action then works to decompose this accumulated matter. The insoluble portion remains on the bottom of the tank, while liquids overflow into a series of disposal lines that are buried beneath the soil, and radiate outward from a central distribution point in various directions.

Called the drainage field, this network of disposal lines consists of large-diameter clay piping laid out so that seepage takes place through the joints between each section. The layout of this drainage field, and the size of the septic tank required, depend on the number of occupants in the house, and on local soil conditions.

Since septic tanks are designed to retain a layer of sludge (decomposed solids) at the bottom, they must be cleaned out periodically to prevent this solid layer from building up sufficiently to cause clogging of the disposal lines, or of the household sewer line. Under ordinary use the tank may need cleaning at two- to four-year intervals, but most experts recommend that the sludge level be inspected every 12 to 18 months. This is accomplished by opening a special manhole cover or trapdoor located at or near ground level. This inspection, as well as cleaning when necessary, is best accomplished by a septic tank serviceman who is trained for the job.

Since grease tends to clog both cesspools and septic tanks, and since it slows up bacterial action in even the best designed tanks, homeowners should avoid pouring fats or oils down the household drain whenever possible. These should be disposed of by storing them in cans, which you then throw out with the kitchen garbage. In large, multiple-family homes, special grease traps are usually installed to catch waste grease before it enters the sewer line.

Some fats and oils will obviously find their way into the waste line from dishwashing or bathing, so you should take steps to dissolve this grease at periodic intervals by using a prepared household drain cleaner. Most of these compounds contain caustic soda, so they must be used with extreme caution according to the directions on the label. Contrary to popular belief, these drain cleaners will not harm septic tanks, or slow up the bacterial action when used in normal amounts. Their action is such that they dissolve the trapped grease in the line, thus preventing a buildup of heavy accumulations.

All Around the House

What can be done to take squeaks out of stairs?
The elimination of annoying squeaks is a job that can almost always be handled by a Ms. Fixit of average skills, equipped with only ordinary hand tools.

Most stair squeaks are caused by a loose tread rubbing against the top of a riser, or against one of the *stringers*, the long wide boards that support the staircase at either side, one against the walls, and the other along the opposite side, under the balusters. You can often silence a slight squeak by squirting powdered graphite or other dry powdered lubricant into the joints between tread and riser, or between tread and stringer. However, this only silences the squeak without eliminating the probable cause: a tread that is loose at some point.

If you want a permanent repair, the loose joints between tread and riser must be tightened up. The easiest method is to drive nails in at an angle. Have someone stand on the offending tread so that his weight holds it down. Then drive two 8d finishing nails into the tread at an angle to each other so that they form a wide V. Space them two or three inches apart, then countersink with a nail set, and fill with matching colored putty.

Treads made of heavy oak or other hardwood are difficult to nail, but you can use screws instead. Drive the screws downward through the tread into the top edge of the riser below. Drill pilot holes first, making them large enough to permit the body of the screw to pass through without difficulty. *Do not drill into the riser.* Use soap or paraffin to help lubricate the screw threads and countersink so that the screwheads can be covered up with wood plugs, or colored putty.

Tightening treads and risers with nails or screws is a method you can usually use on stairs built with a plain butt joint between riser and tread. For those that have been put together with groove-and-rabbet joints, a different method can be used. Thin wooden wedges are driven upward into the loose joint immediately under the stair nosing (the rounded part at the front of the head). If the steps have a molding under the nosing, pry this off first to expose the joint. Then cut thin wooden wedges with your jackknife, coat them with glue, and drive them upward into the recess until they fit snugly. After driving wedges upward till the joint is tight, trim off the surplus wood that sticks down, and renail the cove molding.

To tell whether the stairs in your home are assembled with butt joints or groove-and-rabbet joints, pry off the molding (if there is one), and poke upward with a knife blade along the face of the riser. If solid wood is encountered on the bottom side of the tread, the stairs have butt joints. If there is a crack into which you can slip the knife blade, then the treads and risers are jointed with rabbeted joints.

On cellar stairs, or other stairways where the underside is exposed, there may be wedges between the stringers and risers installed when the stairs were built, but they may have worked loose. If so, they can be tightened by coating them with glue, and hammering them back into place. Drive finishing nails in at an angle after hammering them in as tight as possible.

When looking at the underside of an exposed staircase of this kind, you may find that the bottom edge of a riser has been pushed backward so that it no longer is tight against the back edge of the tread immediately below it. This problem can be quickly set right by hammering the joint shut from behind, then driving nails in at an angle as described above.

Whenever I turn on the washing machine, the pipes bang and rattle as if they were going to come apart. Is there anything that can be done to correct my symphonic plumbing?

A home plumbing system that hammers, bangs, squeals, or creaks every time the water is turned on or off is not only hard on the nerves, it is also hard on the plumbing itself. These noises usually indicate exceptional vibration at some point, and if not corrected in time, may shake mountings and connections loose, and may even cause pipes to burst.

One of the most common noises is a hammering or banging sound heard every time a faucet is suddenly closed. This is caused by the momentum of the fast-moving water when it is slammed to a sudden stop by the closing of a valve. The hammering sound that results is due to the fact that water cannot be compressed, so it bangs around inside the pipe, vibrating back and forth till its forward motion ceases.

In some cases, this condition would not

occur if the pipe were rigidly supported along its entire length so that the pipe itself could not vibrate or give. This is particularly true at elbows and other joints at which the pipe makes a sharp bend, or sudden turn. To check for a potential trouble spot of this kind, inspect all the exposed lengths of pipe. Look for signs of sagging, and for straps or mounting brackets that may have worked loose. Copper water pipes in the $\frac{3}{4}$- and 1-inch sizes should be supported by straps that are spaced no more than eight feet apart. Half-inch pipe should be supported at six-foot intervals.

When checking these supports, pay particular attention to elbows and tees. If possible, there should be a clamp or strap on each side of the elbow, or a wooden block can be installed so that it presses against the side of the pipe just past the turn. For maximum effectiveness, this brace or supporting block should be installed against the piece of pipe on the far side of the turn—in other words, against the side that the water will be hitting as it makes its turn.

A chattering or squealing noise that occurs when a faucet is opened, or when a faucet is left partly open, is usually due to trouble in the faucet itself. The washer on the inside may be loose or badly worn, or the screw that holds the washer in place may have worked loose. Remove the faucet stem as described in the instructions for replacing a faucet washer in Chapter 4, and check the condition of the washer and its retaining screw. If these parts seem tight and in good condition, check the threads on the faucet spindle itself. If they are badly worn, or if there is excessive play when the spindle is in place, chances are that a new faucet will be required in order to eliminate the noise permanently.

A creaking sound coming from a hot water line is usually caused by rapid expansion of the pipe when hot water is drawn into what was previously a cold pipe. The noise may be caused by the pipe rubbing against a beam, or other structural member, as it expands. If this occurs in an accessible location, a cure can be affected by wedging pieces of asbestos, or other heat-resistant fabric, between the pipe and the beam. If this is impractical, the noise can usually be minimized by installation of a spiral expansion coil in the hot water line near the water heater. This coil, which will have to be installed by a plumber, consists of a long length of copper tubing wound into a fairly tight spiral, and sealed off at one end. The other end is connected into the water line close to the heater by means of a suitable connecting tee. The operating principle is much like that of the anti-hammer air chamber just described.

Steam and hot water heating systems may also develop hammering or knocking noises under certain conditions. If this occurs in or near a radiator, particularly in a steam heating system, the trouble may be due to the improper pitch of the radiator. If the radiator slopes the wrong way, accumulated condensation in the form of water will settle at the bottom instead of draining back down through the pipes. To correct this condition, the far end of the radiator—the end away from the inlet valve—should be shimmed up slightly so that the radiator tilts toward the valve. It is suggested that this operation be done by a heating repairman if it requires disconnecting the radiator. But if there is a little play so that you can lift the radiator a fraction of an inch, you can insert the shim yourself. This will expedite drainage of condensed water at the bottom.

Another possible cause of trouble in hot water or steam heating systems is the valve on each radiator. These valves are designed for only one purpose: to turn the radiator off and on. They should never be partly open or partly closed; they should be turned on or off all the way. A partly open valve restricts flow of water or steam into the radiator, and is a frequent cause of hammering or knocking noises in the system.

We recently bought a lovely old house in a hot area of the country, but it doesn't have air conditioning. Should we invest in central air conditioning, which is

both expensive to install and operate, or is there a less costly solution?

You do not need central air conditioning to survive a long, hot summer. Comfort inside the home can be improved considerably through the use of exhaust fans, and an understanding of climate control methods. The chief thing to keep in mind is that moving air is a good deal more comfortable than stagnant air, and that air pulled from a shaded part of the house is cooler than that from a sunny side.

In the summer, temperatures in an attic can climb well over 100°. Since heat flows to cooler areas, it is transmitted through the floors and ceilings to affect all levels of the home. Proper insulation of the attic walls and ceilings, then, will help resist heat absorption from the roof. If your attic is presently uninsulated, you should at least consider installing one of the thin reflective aluminum insulating materials available, even though you won't need it for cold weather protection.

Exhaust fans placed at key locations— kitchen, bathroom, laundry room, and attic —will help remove hot air, and also combat excessive humidity in the home. The simplest arrangement is to use window fans at these locations. A more satisfactory alternative is to install them as wall units vented to the outside via adjustable louvers, which can be shut when not needed.

Intake-exhaust window fans can be used to circulate cooled air through the house. They should be arranged so that air is drawn from a shaded part of the house, and exhausted elsewhere. However, since fans of this type are usually not too powerful, the effective circulation is limited to only a small area.

In many homes—especially one-floor layouts—the best ventilation setup possible is a permanently installed attic fan that can be activated by a wall switch downstairs, or automatically with a combination switch and thermostat. You can have such units installed, or tackle the installation yourself, following directions provided with the unit.

To be effective, the fan must be of a size scaled to your house. It can be mounted centrally in the attic, or anywhere on the attic walls, and it must exhaust to the outside of the house. In addition, vents—or one vent, depending on the layout of the house—must be installed within the house to permit the free flow of air drawn by the fan.

Window air conditioners are available today at fairly reasonable cost. Sometimes one or two of these units can cool a small house if cooled air is helped along with a fan. Naturally, all windows and doors must be kept shut. Also, make certain your electrical wiring will support it.

Like any other piece of equipment, air conditioners need regular servicing to maintain their efficiency. Filters can clog, and impair operation. Depending upon the type of unit, you should clean or replace the filter at the start of the season. If the air conditioner is used extensively, replace the filter mid-season as well. It is good practice to locate the air conditioner on the side of the house that gets the most shade. If this is impractical, a window awning should be installed to put the unit in shade.

The cost of heating fuel rises every year. Besides that, it appears that we will all have to take some steps to conserve fuel. What can we do to get maximum return from our heating dollar?

Let us consider this problem in two parts. First, some general heating tips to supplement the information in Chapter 6. Regardless of the kind of heating you have, certain parts of the system may require an occasional drop or two of oil. This and other maintenance should be mentioned in the manufacturer's instruction booklet.

The temperature you use, like the company you keep, is a matter of personal preference and need. Obviously, the lower the temperature, the less heat needed, and the less fuel burned. Heating costs increase by about three per cent for every degree above 70°.

Now for the second part of the way we tackle the heating problem. Let's take another look at that all important item, the thermostat. About 10 to 15 per cent can be saved on fuel consumption overnight by setting your heating thermostat down at bedtime, and turning it up again the next morning. However, to make savings in this manner, you must keep the following factors in mind as guidance.

Set the thermostat down about 6° or 7° below its daytime setting, but no more. For example, set it no lower than 65° at night if your daytime setting is 72°. A greater reduction of heating does little good, because the heater then has to work overtime the next morning, and burn extra fuel to heat the house up again.

Don't bother with thermostat setback on very cold nights, because little or no savings will result then. The savings are greatest when the outdoor temperature drops to about 30° at night. Savings are less when it goes down to 15° outside, and there is no fuel conserved at 0° or colder. The colder the night, the more fuel required the next morning to reheat the house; this offsets any savings on fuel overnight.

To make any savings at all, your house must be well insulated. The better it's insulated, the greater the night savings. Insulation conserves the heat you start off with in the house when the thermostat is first turned down.

Windows

Our window screens are several years old, and beginning to show their age. Can screens be repaired at home?
When window screens develop loose, wobbly joints, you can reinforce them by screwing metal angle irons or mending plates across the inside corners. Be sure you force the corners tightly together before screws are inserted. If a gap is still visible on the other side, hammer in corrugated metal fasteners to draw the individual frame members together more tightly. These will be scarcely visible from the outside when painted over.

For corner joints that are really weak, or where wood is cracked so that screws will not hold, triangular shaped wooden reinforcing blocks can be screwed and glued to the edges against the inside corner of the weakened frame.

Screen wire made of copper, bronze, or galvanized metal needs periodic painting or varnishing to protect it against corrosion and staining. One of the simplest ways to do this is to lay each screen horizontally across two saw horses, and then paint the wire with a special applicator. This consists of a piece of carpet fastened to the bottom of a wooden, metal, or plastic holder. You can purchase screen wire enamel (in dark green or black), or use thinned down spar varnish.

To apply, pour the paint or varnish into a shallow pan, then dip the carpet applicator into the liquid. Wipe off the excess, then rub briskly over the surface of the mesh on each side. For best results, the molding should be pried off so that the wire underneath can also be painted. When the job is done, nail the molding back into position, countersink the nails, and then fill the holes that remain with putty.

Small holes in metal screens can be patched with ready-made screen patches, or scrap pieces of matching wire mesh. Be sure to use patches of the same kind of metal, or else the two different materials will react chemically, and cause the screen to corrode. Unravel a few wires around all the edges so that about $\frac{1}{2}$ inch of wire is exposed on all sides. Bend these wires at right angles to the surface, and press the patch on over the damaged area, so that the individual wires go through the mesh, and stick out on the inside. Fold these ends in tightly to hold the patch in place; they work much the way as staples holding two sheets of paper together.

Plastic screen that will not hold a crease when folded can be patched with clear plastic cement. Just put a few drops over the holes. You can also darn a plastic or metal patch into place. This works best when the screen has been taken off, laid flat, and the patch placed in position over the hole. Unravel a long strand of the plastic wire, and carefully feed this back and forth through the holes in the screening till you have made a neat and complete patch.

My screens are too badly torn for the repairs you explained. Is there anything I can do short of getting all new ones?
Yes, you can still salvage them. If the wire mesh is badly torn in many places, or so rusted and corroded that cleaning and painting seems hopeless, the only solution lies in recovering with new wire. This task takes time and care, but is reasonably simple, and requires no special tools.

Though there are many different kinds of metal and plastic screening material from which to choose, the handywoman will find that fiberglass insect screening will probably be easiest of all to install. It has a soft, light-weight body that cannot crease or dent, and it is easy to stretch tight by hand. The plastic cuts easily with ordinary household scissors, and once installed, it will never corrode, stretch, or shrink. It never needs painting, either. Fiberglass screening also has excellent visibility qualities, and high resistance to tears and rips.

Begin by prying off the old moldings, working as carefully as possible so that the moldings can be saved for reuse. Next, remove the old screen, and pull out all old tacks or staples.

Now you are ready to put on the new mesh. The problem is to get it tight so that your screens don't look like mesh curtains.

Though the mesh can be pulled tight by hand, the job will be faster and neater if you place 1-inch wooden blocks under each short side of the screen frame after laying it flat on a workbench or table. Then use C-clamps or bar clamps at the midpoint of each long side, clamping the screen frame down to the working surface at its center, so that the entire frame is bowed slightly downward in the middle. If the screening is installed while frames are bowed in this manner, it will be stretched even tighter after the clamps are released.

When you cut the screen mesh to size, allow an extra $\frac{1}{2}$ inch of material on all sides beyond the outside of the molding. This makes a kind of hem, which is folded over under the molding to give a better grip when staples or nails are driven in. Though carpet tacks or small nails can be used, your staple gun, if you have one, will speed the job up considerably. It also makes stretching easier, since only one hand is required for doing the fastening.

After the screening has been cut to size, including the $\frac{1}{2}$-inch excess around the edges, you can proceed as follows:

1. Starting on one of the long sides, tack or staple the mesh into each corner, allowing the excess $\frac{1}{2}$ inch to extend out beyond the molding. Then fasten it in the center, midway between the corners.

2. Fold over the $\frac{1}{2}$ inch of excess, then drive tacks or staples through the doubled thickness at 1-inch intervals. Make sure screening is kept tightly stretched to avoid bunching at any point.

3. Do the opposite long side of the screen next, making certain that the screen wire is pulled tight across the frame. Follow the same procedure as on the first side.

4. Fasten the screening to one of the short sides, then to the other short side, again making certain that the mesh is pulled tight in all directions. If the frame has been clamped in a bowed position as described earlier, remove clamps and block supports. Then replace moldings, using small nails or wire brads.

5. Tap the splines into place on each of the short sides, then use a sharp knife or razor blade to trim off excess screening material on the outside of the spline.

For Your Bookshelf

The you don't need a man to fix it book —The Woman's Guide to Confident Home Repair
by Jim Webb and Bart Houseman, Doubleday and Co., Inc. (New York: 1973)

The Handywoman's Guide
by Michael Squeglia, Henry Regnery Company (Chicago: 1971)

Superhandyman's Encyclopedia of Home Repair Hints
by Al Carrell, Prentice-Hall, Inc. (New Jersey: 1971)

How to Use Hand and Power Tools
by George Daniels, Harper and Row (New York: 1964)

Manual of Home Repair, Remodeling and Maintenance
Grosset and Dunlap (New York: 1972)

The Complete Wise Home Handyman's Guide
by Hubbard Cobb, Thomas Y. Crowell (New York: 1973)

New York Times Complete Manual of Home Repair
by Bernard Gladstone, The Macmillan Company (New York: 1972)

The Householder's Encyclopedia
by Stanley Schuler and Elizabeth M. Schuler, Saturday Review Press (New York: 1973)

I Took a Hammer In My Hand—The Woman's Build-It and Fix-It Handbook
by Florence Adams, William Morrow and Company (New York: 1973)

Practical Electrical and House Wiring
by Herbert P. Richter, Drake Publishers (New York: 1970)

How to Work with Tools and Wood
by Robert Campbell and N. H. Mager, Pocket Book Edition, Simon and Schuster, Inc. (New York: 1972)

Picture Credits

1202 x